THE SOUTHERN WAY

CONTENTS

© Kevin Robertson (Noodle Books) and the various contributors 2009

ISBN 978-1-906419-10-3

First published in 2009 by Kevin Robertson
under the **NOODLE BOOKS** imprint
PO Box 279
Corhampton
SOUTHAMPTON
SO32 3ZX
www.kevinrobertsonbooks.co.uk

Printed in England by
Ian Allan Printing Ltd
Hersham, Surrey

Editorial Introduction

Having the opportunity to indulge one's hobby and turn it into a cottage industry is probably the envy of many and being able to do this with 'Southern Way' is something I will always be grateful for. What makes it even more special is the regular arrival of material, photographs, notes, scans and the like, all of which have made me realise how little in fact I did know of the Southern and how knowledgeable others are.

To be fair, many of us in our hobby probably have an 'expertise' in a specific and limited area, no doubt majoring in a particular field of interest. In many respects this mirrored the professional railwayman, the signal engineers having a knowledge of trackwork but not necessarily the geometry of turnouts, the locomen knowing what to look for but ignorant of bridge design etc etc. Where is all this leading, well just once in a while, one comes across something that indicates a rare grasp of numerous subjects and that took the form of a novel I was loaned recently. How it came into my temporary possession is irrelevant to this narrative, what I will say is that if you ever get the chance to read 'The Memoirs of H. I. Jay - Spook Comes to Stay', subtitled "The Humorous Tales of a Victorian Branch line Stationmaster by his Great-grandson Michael Jay", it is well worth it. Published, I suspect privately in 1990 - ISBN 0-9515354-0-4, it appears to have been the first of three separate books although as far as I can ascertain, only this one appeared. Possibly too and like some, I am slightly wary of fictional accounts of railways and I have to admit it was with not a little trepidation that I agreed to read it.

Set on a fictitious line in Devon, but with definite links with the LSWR, it has all the ingredients of a first rate railway story and from someone who likewise is well versed in both railway history and operation. In fact once I started I could not stop. I subsequently picked up a copy to keep for myself for just £2.00 from an internet site. If you do likewise, I do not think you will be disappointed. (And if per chance someone reading this knows the author, please ask him to get in touch!)

Returning though to the present (- can I actually say that if this is a journal dealing with historic matters….?), I make no excuses that there is a definite 'South Western' influence this time. Yes, I have tried to redress that slightly with the cover view and some other items, but I don't think you will be too disappointed over the quality of what has been submitted. As ever the pile of items to include is greater than the number of available pages but that of course bodes well for the future. I am also in the early stages of thinking about another 'Southern Way - Special' for 2009 as a means of bringing some of this material forward to a wider audience, but timing will depend on how much we can achieve in the autumn months.

Do though keep items coming, whilst I will not make promises I cannot keep as regards when things will appear, I can assure you it will all be used in due course. As ever thank you for your support and encouragement. I heard someone refer to 'SW' as a cross between a book and a magazine the other day, the word he used being 'bookazine'. Perhaps we might even get that included in a future edition of the Oxford Dictionary.

Kevin Robertson

Left: *It is probably some little time since a previously unseen view of one of the two LBSCR steam railmotors appeared, therefore we were delighted with this submission. The general history of these vehicles was very alike that of similar vehicles on other lines. The Brighton cars, built by Beyer Peacock, entered service between Eastbourne and St Leonards on 14th September 1905 and remained so employed until 1912. According to John Minnis, "There is not a lot to give away the location in the photograph but one must assume that it was taken at some point on the east coast line, which traverses flat country throughout much of its length. No 1 has evidently been in service for some time as, when originally built, it had the upper part of the cab painted with cream panels in the same way as the coach. In this guise, it was the subject of numerous photographs, several of them official views. This is the only known view of it in later years when the cab was painted an unrelieved brown. A very interesting find!" After later periods out of use, both had been laid aside by 1919. They eventually ended up in Trindad! (See the RCTS Locos of the LBSCR Part 3 for a detailed history of these vehicles.) Thanks to John Raby, Image: collection of Laurie Rogers.*

Previous page: *The result of enemy action at Victoria, 10.25 pm, 9th October 1940. According to contemporary reports, high-explosive bombs hit the station in the vicinity of Platform 16, damaging three units including the 'Brighton Belle' sets seen here. (Some reports refer to these sets having been painted all over brown in 1940 although obviously this had not been done by this date.) Damage was also occasioned to other stock, whilst bombs hit different parts of the station and also the nearby Grosvenor Hotel. Despite the obvious damage, only two platforms, Nos 16 and 17 were out of use the following morning, probably when this view was taken. All platforms were back in use on 1st November. Spence collection.*

Front cover: *Memories of Victoria, June 1963. 6PAN set No 3026 is destined for a Brighton service, via the Quarry Line. (Victoria in steam days also features in this issue.) Howard Butler*

Rear cover: *34019 'Bideford' on the down through at Eastleigh, unusually displaying the headcode for an engine destined for the depot - not accessible from this line. John Webb.*

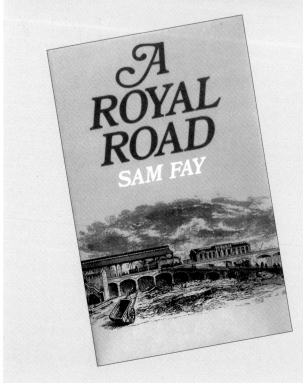

Sam Fay as a child and also circa 1895, approaching 40 years of age. Had the opportunity ever occurred to return to the L&SWR, it is very likely he would have rivalled Walker. Indeed it could well be said Sam Fay was the best General Manager the L&SWR and possibly the Southern Railway never had.

Left - Dust Jacket to the 1973 edition of "A Royal Road". The illustration is of Waterloo Station and Engine House in 1848.

(By kind permission of the Executor of Sir Sam Fay, deceased)

SIR SAM FAY

LONDON & SOUTH WESTERN DAYS

William Fay

An article compiled from diaries and other anecdotal notes left by Sir Sam Fay, relating to his time with the London & South Western Railway between 1872 & 1901

In the latter half of the 19th century railways were the most go ahead and exciting industry to be part of and attracted the ambitious and imaginative young. Sam Fay was just such a young man.

Sam was born at Hamble-le-Rice, in Hampshire on 30th December 1856, his father being bailiff and gardener to the local Rector and later a farmer at Awbridge, in the parish of Michelmersh, near Romsey. The Fay family had farmed at Awbridge since the late 17th century, probably having arrived as Huguenot refugees from France. Sam had the benefit of a basic education at the village school and later, for four years, at Blenheim House School in Fareham, although his elder brother, Charley, was not given this advantage; maybe family circumstances had improved by the time Sam came along.

His first introduction to railways was not auspicious. In later life he recalled a screaming fit on the platform of Blechynden (subsequently Southampton Central) His mother had left him on his own in order to cross the line to buy tickets to Burley and Bournemouth. During the journey her purse, with money and tickets, was stolen!

Sam spoke with a typical Hampshire accent, as exemplified by the late Lord Denning, although it became more muted as his life progressed. In those days local accents were more marked and widespread than they are today. As a youngster he joined a fishing crew, visiting Cornwall where he found the local accent difficult to follow. Again, in 1880, his accent was a problem when he visited Castle Hedingham in Essex. He helped out at the local school by giving dictation – "the young beggars evidently took me for a foreigner, they could not understand what I said".

In 1907 Vanity Fair published a Spy portrait of Mr Sam Fay with the accompanying article saying:

"There is no nonsense about him, but there is an American accent, or, to be exact, it sounds an American accent. It is not. Given the chance, he will assure you with great firmness that he speaks the true Hampshire tongue of which the great American language is but a base and colourable imitation. That tongue, he contends, went to the United States from Poole Harbour and Buckler's Hard; and the Great Republic has striven in vain to live up to it"

He recollected that, in his youth, he "thought it was a fine thing to wear uniform and say "right away" to the guard and engine driver". In those days there was stiff competition for jobs on the railways. Aged 15, Sam was lucky in that his father knew an auditor of the London & South Western Railway and through him he received a coveted nomination to a clerkship from Lewis Ayre, who had been a director since 1835 (i.e. since before the first section of line was opened between Nine Elms and Woking in 1838). His luck held, or more likely he created a good impression for he was quickly selected, subject to passing some comparatively simple mathematical and other tests at Waterloo. These he passed, even though he did not feel he had done himself justice.

Itchen Abbas

So, in 1872 he had his longed for start on the railways as a boy clerk at Itchen Abbas station, learning about passenger and goods station work, including telegraphy and booking clerk's duties. Three months later he became station clerk under the Stationmaster, one Mr Wilmer.

Itchen Abbas was the southernmost station on the Mid Hants Railway, which opened for traffic in October 1865. In Sam Fay's day the line was worked by the L&SWR, who finally bought it in 1884. It closed in 1973 and part of it is now the preserved "Watercress Line". Itchen Abbas is the only station on the line not to have survived.

One of his duties was to operate the bell signal between Itchen Abbas and Winchester Junction (then the junction between the Alton line and the main Waterloo/Basingstoke/Southampton line). This involved giving the signal to the box at the junction and releasing the down starter signal from the ground frame on the platform. Twice he forgot to give the signal and one can

Stockbridge Station and Staff in the early 1900s. No photograph appears to exist from Sam's time but no doubt this would have been a familiar scene to him.

(Photograph kindly provided by Mr Geoff Merritt from his collection)

only imagine the lively language this occasioned at the box when an unannounced train arrived. Rightly this was a serious offence and he received a good "wigging" from Mr Hills, the District Inspector. Luckily he was not dismissed; the Edwardian railway scene would have been poorer without him. Later Hills was to be a Stationmaster under Sam Fay.

Stockbridge

After nine months at Itchen Abbas and a short spell at Alresford, he was transferred to Stockbridge where his duties were the same. Stockbridge was on the Andover and Redbridge Railway (nicknamed the Spratt and Winkle line), which was taken over by the L&SWR in 1861, before completion of the line. It opened to the public in 1865 and closed in 1964. The line, which followed the route of the Andover Canal, was doubled in the years 1883 - 1885.

His new superior was most un-station masterly and Sam thoroughly disapproved of him. His own recollection was:

"There the Stationmaster, whose name was Worsley, son of a clergyman, drank pretty heavily. He had a revolver which he was fond of using to fire at the railings on the platform or at the fire in the porters' room grate. He was short with a big head. I remember a

yokel on the overbridge by the station telling him during a backchat when Worsley was fresh *(from drink)* "go on, you've got to grease your head to get your shirt on." Worsley was a bachelor, his sister keeping house for him, a very refined lady who had to put up with his unpleasant moods."

Although not averse to a drink himself Sam was saddened by the drunkenness which was prevalent in the mid 19th century. Writing in a more sober age he recalled that it was a common sight to see men and women reeling about the streets, especially on a Saturday night. He had memories of many promising careers ruined or cut short by drink. No doubt he would be horrified to recognise the scenes of drunkenness, now aggravated by drugs, commonplace in our town centres today.

At Stockbridge they had a porter, nicknamed "Coppertop" who, not one of the brightest, was a constant source of entertainment to the other staff. On one occasion he was sent to ask the engine driver for the keys to the tunnel. Sam did not report the driver's response beyond "unprintable".

His L&SWR staff record shows he moved, in February 1875, to Turnham Green and later in the year to Southampton. His own records show this as a period he spent on the relief staff working at various stations up

The Railway Station, Kingston.

Kingston buildings and train shed from the station approach.

(Lens of Sutton collection - 86186)

and down the line, filling in for temporary vacancies or for those absent for leave or illness. So maybe he was nominally attached to Turnham Green and Southampton while actually working as relief at nearby stations.

Kingston-upon-Thames

In 1876 Sam was appointed a clerk at Kingston-upon-Thames station. This was to be a more settled period, during which he courted and married Frances Farbrother. We are fortunate that he kept diaries from January 1878 to July 1881, part of his time at Kingston. They give some insight into the life of a young ambitious railway clerk at the time and end when his own efforts were bringing him to the attention of senior managers and directors of the L&SW R.

In that era Kingston was the County Town of Surrey and an Assize Town. Sam had occasion to attend the courts on railway business, he mentions two cases involving passengers opening doors first on the wrong side of the train and secondly when the train was not in the station. A not uncommon experience in an era when railways were still a novelty. Neighbouring Surbiton had only just started to grow around the Waterloo/ Southampton line and had been a small village, the station there had been the original Kingston Station.

This line had been opened in two parts, firstly

from Twickenham to Kingston in 1863 and then from Coombe (later Malden for Coombe) to Kingston in 1869 to tap into the increasing population of the area. Mr C Pettit was the Station Master and Sam evidently respected him, obviously a "proper Station Master". Pettit seems to have been a paternalistic manager for when Sam was ill Pettit went to see him every day and even sent him "baked apples and pudding". There were three clerks when Sam started at Kingston, of which he was a junior up to December 1879 when the senior clerk, one Osborne, was transferred to Windsor Goods. Sam took Osborne's place and his salary (or "screw" as he referred to it) was increased to £80 per annum. It appears from the diaries, that Hampton Wick also fell under the control of Kingston as he was sent there as relief clerk regularly. At times Kingston was "deuced" busy for the ticketing clerk, he records 1,480 passengers in a day and 1,200 in an afternoon on 23rd April and 10th June 1878 and 23,000 passengers for July that year and 25,000 the following July – "Best month we have ever had here". At the same time as dealing with passengers the clerks were responsible for a not inconsiderable parcels traffic.

The third clerk, Damen, was responsible for goods traffic and when he went on leave Sam took on his work as well – "This goods relief is rather too much of a good thing". Osborne and Fay worked either a morning, 5 a.m. to 1 p.m. shift or 1 p.m. to 9 p.m. evening, shift. Which duty, they were on, depended on local arrangements but this was regularised in April 1878 When Scott, the General Manger, decreed that, where there were two, one clerk must work a week of mornings and the other a week of evenings alternatively. Sam commented that this change "does not meet general approval". This came about when Gooden, a clerk at Putney, reported late one morning, missing the first train of the day about 5 a.m.. Scott threatened him with resignation if this recurred. The hapless clerk protested asking how he could be expected to get up when his last train was 12pm (the previous night).

It was common then for lowly clerks, away from home to live in lodgings. Initially Sam lodged with a Mrs Redfern who provided him with breakfast, "a rasher and cocoa", and evening meal. At first he appears to have been quite content with this but in July 1878 he gave notice because "I can't stay here with that fool of a Compton" (more about Compton, a bookstall clerk later). He found alternative lodgings in East Road but "Mrs Redfern has taken it so to heart my leaving, that I have given them up". By November 1881 matters had deteriorated and he did move:

"Mon. 22nd. Cleared out of my lodgings at Mrs Redfern's, The Bookstall clerk Davis also left, things have been going on very rough here lately, bad dinners and worse cooking, late hours kept by the inmates keeping us awake, and last but certainly not the least objectionable feature, the anything but moral conduct of Mrs R's niece."

His new lodgings were a bedroom in Shanklin Villa, Richmond Park Road, costing 4s (20p!) per week, and having his meals in a local tavern. This was not a good move. – "12th February I have got a nasty attack of the "Shingles" and am in the doctor's hands, I believe my damp bedroom has something to do with it". Happily he was soon to find more congenial surroundings. His friend Walter Farbrother was married in early March and Sam went to live with the newlyweds at 13, Albert Road, Norbiton – "My new room is a treat looking straight across the Fairfield."

This Walter was the brother of Frances Farbrother who he was courting at the time and who he was to marry in 1883. She and Walter were the children of a local cabinet maker and undertaker. On many occasions Sam records helping Walter, either being a pallbearer or assisting in collecting a dead body, by horse drawn hearse, from as far away as St Georges Hospital Hyde Park Corner.

Two of Frances and Walter's nephews, Charles Farbrother and William Farbrother were later to join the L&SWR, ending up as Southern Railway Station Masters at Cosham and Bournemouth respectively. No doubt Sam had some influence on both careers.

It is unclear as to whether he met Frances through Walter or, perhaps more probably through the landlady, Mrs Redfern. She was certainly a friend of the latter's (and they may have been related) as they had a short holiday together. Courting seems to have involved many a long walk, occasional dances and regular church attendance – "To Ham Church in the evening. Mr Hough preached a beautiful sermon; he must be a good man".

Apart from courting and walking Sam spent much of his spare time on sporting activities. Rugby football features but his favourite winter pastime was skating on local ponds and lakes which froze over most winters. The winter of 1878/79 was particularly good for skaters if not for the railways. On Christmas Eve – "trains very late, two engines failed thro' the bursting of the pipes with frost" and on Boxing Day "the river has been frozen over above Kingston Bridge but not enough to bear".

Rowing was, however, his favourite sport, pursued through most of the year. It certainly appealed to his competitive streak. The Kingston Rowing Club thrives today and it did so in Sam's time. From his diaries it is apparent that many local clerks were members of the club and he was put up for membership by his senior clerk and good friend, Osborne, being elected on 20th March 1878. Seven months later he was on the committee, his first management experience.

He rowed as often as his duties allowed. "For row in a four to Swan and back, got on first rate" and "For a scull in the morning". His intended was, however, not so keen – "Trottie (a family name for Frances Farbrother) doesn't like this rowing business because it keeps me away from her till rather late" and again "I did not go to see her till after nine o'clock, she thought I was drowned". Evidently his rowing was a cause of friction between them!

Sam was a useful rower but perhaps not top notch, seemingly often coming second in finals. His excuse was that he did not get enough practice but this is a little hard to believe seeing as he records being on the water so often. The prizes certainly motivated him – "Am going in strong for the sculling prize (an epergne)" and referring to the medal on offer for the fours: "I *must* (his italics) have one of them" In presenting him with the cup for second in the Junior Sculls the Mayor of Kingston said that he hoped Sam (age 21) would long live to drink champagne out of it. He did, for another 75 years.

Rowing was not all hard work. The club ended the season with a dinner which can only be described as magnificently Victorian; his diary for 30th October, 1878 records:

'O2' No 363 at Hounslow circa 1905. During Sam's time with the LSWR this station was known as 'Hounslow for Whitton'. The headcode refers to a Twickenham - Gunnersbury service and which in steam days was served by slightly more than one train per hour Monday to Saturday. On Sundays the service was Feltham to Gunnersbury with 13 trains between 8.30 am and 10 30 pm. First and Third class accommodation only was provided on these services. Interesting there is a prominence of posters advertising Paris as a destination.

"To our Rowing Club dinner at the Sun Hotel, the Mayor in the chair, had a capital dinner, I first of all performed on some turbot and oyster sauce, then stewed eels, turkey and sausages, a leg of fowl, a half a partridge, then some hare, jelly, cheese and celery, finishing with dessert; a bottle of Hock, 2 quart bottles of pale ale, 2 bottles of champagne between four of us; the speeches and songs were very good, about 50 dined, it was a very select party, the dinner was 6s (30p in today's money, but not value) a head without wine, but after cashing up the sum total of my feed I fear the Landlord Mr J Bond did not get very much out of me"

One can only hope that the present members of Kingston Rowing Club get to enjoy such a feast!

As well as his work, rowing and courting Sam took a great interest in current events. His diaries record in some detail two visits to see the House of Commons in action; a place he would get to know very well in supporting and opposing many railway bills. Tickets of admittance had to be obtained from a member and Sam's father got them for him from William Cowper-Temple, MP for South Hampshire, who lived at Broadlands, subsequently to be the Mountbatten home. Cowper-Temple is best known for steering through

Platform 3 (right) at Waterloo. The centre line continued on to form the connection with the SE & CR.

parliament the Bill which led to the construction of the Thames Embankment in London.

Of course what he recorded reflected the times. The second Afghan War and Russian expansionist aims in the Balkans feature, as does the Zulu War of 1879. Regarding the latter he recorded news of the disastrous battle of Isandhlwana with the loss of 500 men of the 24th Regiment – "great excitement in consequence" and a day later – "A large number of troops have been ordered to the Cape. Mr Zulu had better look out". In the event he was right and the Zulus were defeated. It was in this war that Prince Napoleon, son of the exiled Napoleon III, was killed, age 23 – "he was cowardly left by his comrades". Sam evidently saw this as a great event and went, by train, to Chislehurst to see the funeral procession which was a sight he would never forget. The cortege must have been quite magnificent, almost a state funeral, with the coffin on a gun carriage drawn by eight horses, followed by many a Prince, the military and a great number of French, the whole topped and tailed by squadrons of lancers. He was also prescient following the First Boer War, which followed – "We have managed to come to terms.........thus laying in a crop of troubles in the future"

The following year was one of excitement over the general election, returning the Liberal Gladstone as prime minister. In early March Sam had gone to a meeting at the Assize Courts addressed by the two Liberal candidates for Mid Surrey (Stern and Higgins). A mob attempted to put their champion, a stonemason on the platform but in the attempt the gas pipe was broken bringing the meeting to a premature halt. Sam, at that time was evidently a Tory supporter; later in life he became a staunch Liberal. A few years later he was elected to Kingston Council whether as a Tory or Liberal is unclear, or maybe as an independent as independents in local government were far more common then. His reaction to Gladstone's victory appears very jingoistic, probably reflecting the age – "goodbye to English patriotism and England's supremacy throughout the world." His thoughts on Disraeli's death, the next year, were in similar vein but did touch on his own ambitious views and the optimism of Victorian times – "his (Disraeli's) career must act as a stimulus to many a young man trying to rise in the world."

His diary entries did not ignore railway events. The late 1870s and 1880s were a time of depression in agriculture and industry to which the railways were not immune. Indeed industrial unemployment, for the first time, became a major issue. He makes reference to the strike of Midland Goods guards against a reduction in pay in January1879. In the same month Scott, the L&SWR General Manager, resisted pressure, from his directors and the other companies, to lower staff wages and also to add the 5% government duty to season tickets. This was a tax levied on passenger fares at the time and it appears that the L&SWR bore the cost of this as far as season ticket sales were concerned.

Sam was certainly not lacking in ambition and comments on this in his diary:

"Read "Harold" (by Lord Lytton) again this morning, methinks my nature is somewhat the same as his, at least as to ambition, but we are all ambitious there surely can be no sin in it, my fancy takes very high flights at times, building castles in the air that I know never will be realised, in sober moments my thoughts plan out my future, they make me chief clerk at some good station then with my darling Trottie, in charge of a small country station and eventually a large one"

He did not record what the "castles in the air" were but they were probably more accurate than his "sober" thoughts as he never did become a Station Master, more like a Master of Station Masters on the L&SWR and Master of the Railway on the Great Central.

In the diaries he mentions many changes in clerical staff up and down the line. Sam applied for a few of these. He reports on one of these occasion Mr Pettit's written recommendation "He is a good clerk, and I shall be sorry to loose him, but I must not stand in his way to keep him back, I have therefore much pleasure in recommending him for the position for which he asks". Sam's reaction is a fairly brusque "He could not say much more and he could certainly not say less"!

Interestingly many of the staff changes seem to be brought about by misdemeanours or fraud by clerks, for example:

"I hear that Mr Greig, who used to be at Surbiton, cashier at Nine Elms has defrauded the company to the tune of about £1,000" (about £85,000 at today's values),

"I hear that my friend Guyatt at Kensington has resigned. He was suspended for swearing at the clerk in charge", and

"Benning at Southampton Docks has I hear gone wrong for a thousand, a good help to the guarantee"

In one instance he recorded that, at Wimborne: "Gale put in a Lunatic Asylum"!

Ambitious he may have been but he did not lack generosity. When his father hit hard times with the farm Sam turned over to him all the savings he had in the Southampton Savings Bank and two or three pounds a month out of his pay (about 40%). He was also generous to friends in need. A bookstall clerk at

Kingston, one Haycock, was desperate for cash and could not raise it elsewhere. "The young fool has lost it betting and card Playing". Sam lent him £9, having himself borrowed some of the amount from his manager against a promissory note. Sam was not optimistic of the loan being repaid fearing "He will go to the bad in the end". Within a week Haycock tried to borrow a further "sovereign" but Sam was not that generous! Repayment was promised in six weeks time. A year later he had not been repaid and he does not record if it ever was.

Probably today he would be described as a company man, he was certainly loyal to his employers. When another bookstall clerk, Compton, pinched some used tickets to take himself and four others to Waterloo, Sam (together with Osborne) turned him in to Pettit and Compton was forced to pay up. Quite obviously this generated ill feeling between them, not made any easier by their both lodging with Mrs Redfern at the time. He took pride in his work and did not have any problems with his monthly cash returns to head office or with the regular audits.

As well as copious staff changes he takes an interest in what was happening elsewhere on the L&SWR, for instance the opening of the Aldershot and Ascot line, the quadrupling of the main line between Surbiton and Woking and a number of railway accidents. These ranged from a comparatively simple "engine off at Richmond in evening, blocked the up line for several hours" to the more serious "bad accident on our line at the Loco Junction at Nine Elms, five or six killed and a lot injured". This accident happened, in torrential rain, when the 10.01 p.m. train, hauled by the engine "Firefly", from Cyprus Station (the south station, part of the sprawl of the original Waterloo) ran into a goods engine standing on the main line and waiting to enter Nine Elms locomotive depot. After striking the goods engine the train continued in the six foot for 110 yards, the first carriage ended on top of "Firefly" and, according to 'The Times', several other coaches were "smashed to atoms and reduced to matchwood". There was little damage to the heavy goods engine and it's crew were uninjured but "Firefly's" fireman, James Arnott was killed along with five passengers. The driver, Samuel Taylor died later from his severe injuries. Major Marindin's report to the Board of Trade blamed the accident on the signalman, Almond and the boy (presumably a pupil signalman), Kempson, forgetting they had a stationary loco standing on the main line. (Shades of Quintinshill to come in May 1915). The Board of Trade report, not for the first or last time, recommended the installation of continuous train brakes, Major Marindin was of the opinion that this would have reduced the speed of "Firefly" and it's train, at the time of impact from 30 to 10 mph thus preventing the loss of life.

PROSPECTUS.

"The South Western Gazette."

LONDON, MAY 5TH, 1881.

On the 1st of next month, and on the 1st of each succeeding month, it is proposed to publish the **"South Western Gazette,"** a paper devoted exclusively to matters affecting the South Western Railway. The price to be one penny.

The profits will be handed over to the **Widows' and Orphans' Fund.**

The principal features of the **"Gazette"** will be as follows :—

A list of the promotions and appointments in all branches of the service : both in salaried and uniform staff.

Short articles on matters affecting the South Western Railway.

Local notes from all Stations.

Personal recollections of former Superintendents, Station Masters, &c.

A History of the South Western Line is also promised.

Correspondents are respectfully invited from all Stations.

It has been thought that a paper such as this would be interesting to all S. W. men, and that by the exchange of ideas it would create a good feeling between all classes in the service.

May we—the promoters of the **"Gazette"**—ask you, in the interest of the **Widows' and Orphans' Fund,** to kindly canvass your clerks and men for orders, and forward the same to the Secretary of the South Western Company's Institute and Club, Brunswick House, Vauxhall, not later than the 14th inst., together with any suggestions of your own for increasing the popularity and usefulness of **"The Gazette."**

Upon receipt of the first number we should be glad if you would collect the pence from the subscribers for the following three months, and forward the same to the Institute at your earliest convenience.

Any Local Notes from your Station for our first number will be especially welcome. If you favour us with any copy during this, or any other month, please to send it in five days *at least* before the end of the month.

W. H. GOFFE.
S. FAY.
H. DYER.

The weather was to blame for a couple of other accidents. Snow blocking the up main signal at West London Junction resulted in a train of empty carriages running into a Goods and also fog at Woking caused a smash between the Southampton and Exeter Goods trains; "Smashed up a rare lot of trucks".

For those who like to know details of station changes; he records - 18th April 1881 – "More alterations being made on the High Level Station here (Kingston), the slope to the down main and the steps to the up are to be covered in, together with a part of each platform, the latter are to be raised several inches"

Apart from being provided with a good basic education Sam Fay rose to senior railway management by his own efforts. In mid 1881 he brought about the event which first introduced him to the senior management and the directors of the L&SWR. Whether or not this was his intention is not known. In his own words:

"Thu. 28th May: I have an idea that a paper called the S.W. Gazette devoted to matters affecting the S.W.R. and giving the promotion and changes in the staff would take well if the profits were handed over to the Widows' and Orphans' fund. I saw Goffe (a clerk in the General Manager's office) about the idea this evening, he agrees with me and proposes to start on June 1st."

With typical Sam energy events moved quickly. The next day they enlisted Dyer, the secretary of the S.W. Institute and Club, started to put together a programme and wrote to L&SWR agents in the country seeking contributions. A prospectus (see opposite) was produced within a week and printers engaged, "on very good terms". A print run of 500 was anticipated. By the middle of the month Correspondents were agreed for Exeter and Southampton and others promised articles. On the 21st May they "Got a great deal of the copy down to the printers. 1,100 orders in". 2,000 were ordered from the printer on 31st May which were despatched the next day. A week later they ordered 350 more and, significantly, Sam comments: "The directors are very pleased with it and have bought several copies". At the end of June the second edition was sent out with a total order of 2,400.

Sam's diaries end at this point. He must have found his spare time fully taken by the South Western Gazette and his next project. The prospectus for the Gazette shows a history of the South Western Line as being promised. He duly wrote this, with the help and encouragement of a friend, William Drewett, a Kingston printer and former editor of the "Surrey Comet". It was published as a book, under the title "A Royal Road" in 1882 (A facsimile edition was published in 1973). He always felt that this 'little book' was responsible for his subsequent railway career.

From these events he learned the value of publicity and would use it to great effect in his time on the Great Central. That is outside the scope of this article but those who wish to pursue the thread should refer to the third volume of George Dow's excellent history of the Great Central, aptly subtitled "Fay Sets the Pace".

Before we move on from Kingston a couple of anecdotes, which Sam left us, are worth recording. The pay of railway clerks was poor and a number of them got together, making Sam their secretary.

He produced a petition to the Directors which was presented through the General Manager. Having obtained an interview they had to wait some time at

Waterloo. During this wait one of their number had a drink or two, no doubt for dutch courage. "We all got increases in pay except the clerk who looked upon the wine when it was red". This was in the days when trade unions were in their infancy.

> 21. Should any Servant think himself aggrieved, he may memorialise the Board; but in any such case the memorial must be sent through the head of his department. Memorials ought not to be addressed to individual Directors, but to the Board.

From the 1864 L&SWR Rules and Regulations.

During one of the Directors annual inspections of the line, a saloon was requested. Because of a telegraphic error a fine Salmon was provided, much to their amusement.

Waterloo & Nine Elms

In 1884 he was asked by the Superintendent of the Line, E.W. Verrinder, to join his office, and a year later was appointed Chief Clerk. His boss was evidently not an easy man to get along with, nevertheless Sam remained in his office for seven years. He recorded that Verrinder "had an idea that scowling at an employee was the best way of enforcing discipline. He went around the office at Waterloo and strafed everyone for errors never committed".

Matters came to a head with Verrinder when one of Sam's subordinates was appointed a District Superintendent. He objected on the grounds that the appointment should have been his, and appealed to the General Manager. The upshot was his appointment as Assistant Stores Superintendent at Nine Elms.

He recalled, concerning the General Manager Archibald Scott "At 11 a.m. every morning it was the custom to have a refresher in the shape of a pint of beer. I often found myself standing at the refreshment counter between a porter and Archibald Scott, the General Manager. Mr Scott's drinking habits were peculiar. He frequently left the refreshment room by one door to enter by another, then take a second draught".

M&SWJR

He remained at Nine Elms for nine months, before getting his first taste of real management power. The small Midland and South Western Junction Railway was in severe difficulties and in receivership. The directors of the line asked Charles Scotter, who had succeeded Scott as General Manager, if he could recommend someone to take on the post of Secretary and General Manager of the M&SJR. He did: Sam Fay, who was interviewed and accepted the position.

Sam had previously applied for the vacant Manager position of the Waterford and Central Ireland

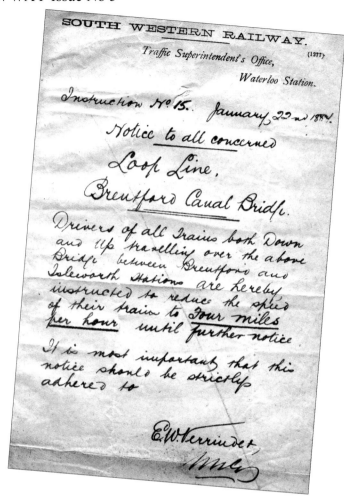

Railway, being recommended by the senior management of the L&SWR. He was interviewed at Kilkenny by the Directors. However the prospects did not appeal to him, he made his excuses and declined the post, "glad to escape from an uncomfortable position…."

The M&SWJR is outside the scope of this article. It is sufficient to record that he succeeded in putting the line on a sound footing and removed it from receivership. At the end of his time there it is said that a local Cheltenham Newspaper editor commented that Sam "had made an empty sack stand upright". On a personal level he felt that his seven years at Cirencester were amongst the happiest of his life.

In his leaving speech, as reported in the Gloucester Standard, Sam gives fulsome praise to the railwaymen, managers and directors in their unity and cohesion. This touches on one of his significant abilities as a manager, the ability to put together a strong team and to lead and support it. This would be demonstrated again in his days on the Great Central.

In his absence Verrinder had died in July 1893 and been succeeded as Superintendent by GT White. When he too died in March 1899 Sam returned to the L&SWR, taking up the appointment of Superintendent of the line under the General Manager, Charles Scotter. Incidentally Scotter, like Sam Fay, rose from junior clerk to become a General Manager. He came up through the ranks of the Manchester, Sheffield & Lincolnshire Railway (later Great Central Railway) to Goods Manager, leaving after 32 years to take up his position with the L&SWR.

During his time as Superintendent one of the significant events was the introduction of low pressure pneumatic signalling to British railways. This had its origin in an inspection visit he made to New York in 1899, during which he was shown such signalling in use at Grand Central Station. He reported positively to the General Manager and the company decided to trial it at Grateley. The work included replacing the original two signal cabins by a single one on the up platform. It was undertaken by a newly formed company; the British Pneumatic Railway Signal Co. Incidentally this company's "outdoor assistant", presumably equivalent to today's Site Engineer, was one Arthur Bound, who was to go on to be one of the leading signal engineers of his day, with GCR, LNER and finally as Chief Signal and Telegraph Engineer of the LMS.

The installation was opened, with due fanfare, on 31st July, 1901. Amongst those attending were: JT Allen, Assistant Superintendent (later Superintendent) of the Line of the GWR, HG Drury, Superintendent of the Line of the GER and J Alexander of the GNR, whose duties it has not been possible to establish, as well as luminaries of the L&SWR, including Dugald Drummond, and the contractors. The celebrations involved much champagne, Sam's recollection was "the waiters got drunk and rolled out underneath the tent. A local paper said I was as bright and smiling as the morning itself".

Waterloo had grown, haphazardly but following a report by Sam Fay to the directors Waterloo Station was to be rebuilt and enlarged The new station was finally opened in 1922 and then stood largely unaltered until Waterloo International was opened in 1994.

One of the duties of the Superintendent was to travel in charge of royal trains. The Prince of Wales (subsequently Edward VII) once complained about his breakfast getting cold, it having been sent to Waterloo in a hay box to keep it warm. To improve matters Sam had

The South Station concourse at Waterloo, possibly after 1902.

(Spence collection)

South Station at Waterloo.

a coal gas oven installed on the train. On arrival at Southampton the foreman footman sought out Sam saying "see what you have done to me". The poor chap had allowed the gas to build up in the oven before lighting it. His eyebrows were burnt and his hair singed. The prince, however had not noticed being too busy with his fish, eggs and bacon!

Sam Fay had a competitive nature and was a believer in improving and speeding up services in order to compete with neighbouring lines, something he was to do successfully for the Great Central. In 1899 he ran a trial train from Waterloo to Bournemouth, completing the 108 miles in 110 minutes. His instinct was to boost Bournemouth, as a seaside resort, in competition with Brighton. The day after this run he was sent for by the Chairman and told "Don't do it again Sam, not in my lifetime". Apparently his Chairman had been on the train and was rather shaken by the hard riding.

The London and South Western had considerable experience of working with the military in view of the number military establishments in its area. Sam's first encounter with the War Office did not impress him. He recalls in "The War Office at War", his World War I memoirs, that in 1886, while on Verinder's staff, there were fears of civil unrest in the capital. The L&SW was ordered to put on a train to move a regiment from Portsmouth to London. The train was provided but

the regiment never appeared. Sam was sent to the War Office to sort this out. He was met by total indifference by the officers, both civil and military. In the end "I rapped the desk of one individual who did not look up when told of my errand, and demanded to see the Quartermaster-General". He was eventually told to cancel the train and commented that the War Office may have found the regiment, but the railway never did.

By the time he was next to experience the War Office, the latter had improved immensely. He worked closely with them throughout the Boer War as most of the troops and equipment for the campaign were shipped through Southampton. The L&SW acquitted themselves well, being able to supply and operate all necessary trains and dock facilities. Sam recorded that in the first seven months of the war the railway transported 212,370 officers and men, 27,000 horses and 1,186 wagons and other vehicles; felt to be a great feat at the time. This experience stood him on good stead when he was appointed to the War Office during the Word War I when vastly more men and military materials had to be shipped from and to UK shores.

After the L&SWR

At the end of 1901 the Great Central Railway needed a new General Manager to replace Sir William Pollitt. Their chairman Alexander Henderson, later Lord Farringdon wanted Sam Fay for the post and he accepted. The L&SWR did not wish to see him go and he was warned off the position by Colonel Williams, one of their directors – "The Great Central will be in Receivership before the year is out. I am their banker, I know". Sam was aware of the GCR's position but did not believe it to be quite that serious. His faith was justified and under his management the GCR batted well above its position in the railway league.

Leaving the L&SWR was, however, not the last of his connections to what was to become the Southern Railway. He had been asked, in 1902, by Sir John Blundell Maple MP, son of the founder of Maple's furniture store, to value the Isle of Wight railways. Not an easy job as none of the three lines paid. Sir John's intention was to purchase land and the railways with a view to developing the island. He made a start by acquiring a majority of shares in the Freshwater, Yarmouth & Newport line. When, the following year, Sir John died his executors sold the shareholding to Frank Aman, who had hotel and land interests at Totland Bay, and Sam Fay. Aman took a seat on the board and played a significant part in directing the company. Sam contributed much professional advice and played a major part in 1913 when the Freshwater, Yarmouth & Newport took back the running of the line from the Isle of Wight Central Railway. He took a leading role in negotiations with the Isle of Wight Central, recruited suitable management (the new General Manager came from the Great Central Railway), and arranged for the purchase of locos and rolling stock. The company was always stretched for cash and Sam Fay, with Frank Aman, was appointed joint receiver in 1913. The company never paid a dividend but Sam expressed himself as very satisfied with the capital payment received in 1923 from the Southern.

He retired from active railway management, upon grouping, at the end of 1922, having served at the War Office during the Kaiser's War, latterly as Director General of Movements and Railways, a position which gave him a seat on the army council. Grouping did not see the end of Sam Fay's railway interests (by then he had become Sir Sam, being knighted by George V at the opening of Immingham Docks in July 1912). He continued to be an active director of two Argentine railways and was Chairman of locomotive builders: Beyer Peacock from 1923 to 1933.

Sam Fay died on 30th May 1953. What great changes he had seen in his beloved railways. He is buried at Awbridge in Hampshire, having returned to the land of his ancestors in 1923, when he bought a substantial property, Awbridge Danes. Family legend has it that, in his youth, he had worked there as a boot boy, swearing that one day he would own it. Myth it may be but it does ring true to his character.

Acknowledgements.

I am, of course, very grateful to Sir Sam Fay for leaving us his Kingston diary and other writings. He had had some idea of writing his autobiography, but sadly this never happened. What a mine of information *and insights into railway management that would have been. I am grateful to my father, His Honour Judge Edgar Fay Q.C., for turning over to me various Sam Fay papers, and also for his permission, as Sir Sam Fay's surviving Executor, to quote from these and from Sam's publications.*

I must also thank Geoff Merritt for the photograph of Stockbridge station and Audrey Giles of Kingston University for providing me with a copy of Sam Fay's L&SWR staff record.

Kevin Robertson inspired me to write this article and my thanks are due to him for his assistance and encouragement. The errors are mine, not his.

An extremely useful source of additional information has been 'The Times' on line archive. I would thoroughly recommend this to anyone searching for contemporary newspaper accounts and obituaries.

The following books have also proved useful to me in providing background information:-
Colin G Maggs -
'Branch Lines of Hampshire'
'The Midland & South West Junction Railway'
RJ Maycock & R Silsbury –
'The Freshwater, Yarmouth & Newport Railway'
Sam Fay - 'A Royal Road'
Sir Sam Fay – 'The War Office at War'

I can also recommend George Dow's 'Great Central, Vol. 3' which covers Sam Fay's GCR career. In writing this article I have studiously avoided rereading this book as George Dow had access to some of the same source material and I wanted to avoid the trap of using his phraseology, even unconsciously.

'415' class 4-4-2T No 129 at Waterloo. Built in October 1885 it is displaying the headcode for a Waterloo to Guildford service, via Cobham.

BRIDGE OVER THE RIVER TORRIDGE

Rod Garner

As is invariably the way, as soon as a book appears then out of the woodwork more material will emerge. Such was the case with these three views associated with Rod Garner's TORRINGTON & MARLAND LIGHT RAILWAY (Kestrel Railway Books).

The views all relate to the construction of the viaduct over the River Torridge in preparation for the rebuilding of the T & M as the North Devon and Cornwall junction Light Railway, which connected Torrington with Halwill Junction.

Above - Looking away from Torrington over the River Torridge, the masonry piers for the new viaduct stand awaiting the steel bridgework, probably in May 1923. During the winter floods of 1924, the foundations of one of the piers were undermined by the river. Instead of starting again with the pier, it was winched back into position and underpinned to a foundation ring blasted out of the river bed. This was probably the pier in the river closest to the camera in this shot. Behind the new piers is, of course, J.B.Fell's old Marland timber viaduct built for the 3 foot gauge Torrington & Marland Light Railway. At the time, the narrow gauge line was still in everyday use for clay traffic, although as construction of the N.D.C.J.L.R. proceeded, some construction traffic used the T & M line as well. The low level structure in between the two is the contractor's staging used as access in building the piers. It is possible that temporary rails were laid over this during the construction period, to enable materials to be delivered directly to where the piers were being built. (See also Page 45 of LINES TO TORRINGTON by John Nicholas.)

BRIDGE OVER THE RIVER TORRIDGE
Rod Garner

A view up the Pencleave Valley towards Watergate with the first set of girders in place and finishing-off work being completed. The gentleman on the left appears to be heating up rivets in his portable forge, while his two colleagues stand by to receive the hot metal. Note that all three men are wearing suits and flat hats. This span is the first which carries the line over the Rolle Road and has the girders set higher than those over the river. Here the line runs within the girders; over the river it is carried on the side girders.

Health & Safety considerations do not appear to rate highly in this scene, although the handrails are already fitted to the main span! Latterly, a second and higher set of handrails was fitted outside the originals. Note the pole and ladder tied overhead, with what appears to be a tarpaulin draped over it to cover the working area. The work appears to have been carried out by Braithwaite's of West Bromwich, a firm of structural engineers. Apparently some unspecified parts of the steelwork for the bridge were damaged whilst being unloaded at Halwill. Rather than replacing the damaged parts, the rivets were drilled out, the damaged parts straightened and then re-riveted! The source of the smoke in the far background would appear to be a train on the narrow gauge line, working bunker first towards Torrington.

Above - The new viaduct is complete and track on the old bridge has been disconnected. This interesting view was probably taken soon after the opening of the N.D.C.J.L.R. on 27th July 1925. Note that double check rails were provided over the bridge. Compare the differences in height and gradients of the two bridges and notice the pronounced dip in the old bridge on the first of the main spans. The narrow road running under the bridges this side of the river is the bed of the old Rolle Canal, now the Rolle Road. The completed bridge was 700' long and 40' high and at the time of opening, was referred to in the Press as "Opening up a new area in the west".

Right - The Watergate end of the same bridge 80+ years later and now part of the 180 mile 'Tarka Trail', which covers much of North Devon, including the course of several closed lines. The pronounced kink between the two spans, is much more than on any of the others. Was this deliberate, due to the 'new' bridge running inside the old one and being of a slightly tighter radius, or down to a bit of 'bend it in at the end, it'll be alright'?
The newly formed "Tarka Valley Railway' is also based at nearby Torrington and expect to have laid its first track panels by the end of 2008. (The TVRG Membership Secretary, The Puffing Billy, Torrington Station, Station Hill, Torrington, Devon, EX38 8JD.)

CONUNDRUMS

Conundrum indeed, or I suppose we could refer to the conjoined 'Signal & Telegraph' department. The view was taken at Stone Crossing Halt near Dartford in the early to mid 1960s. Is it unique? Or were there other such examples? Obviously not destined to survive for much longer either, as witness the MAS bracket in the background. Thanks to Joe Cussen for sending it to us.

BASINGSTOKE

Part 2 - Rebuilt and Expanded

Roger Simmonds

(Continued from Southern Way No 3)

'One of the most modern stations in the United Kingdom'. So extolled Mr. Szlumper, the LSWR Engineer, on the completion of the new facilities in 1904. Such was the extent of the work and the inherent need for purchasing additional land, that activities had prevailed for six full years. The LSWR had been faced, not only with acquiring land to the South and West of the old station but also in negotiating the re-housing of many families of the 'labouring classes' with both the Local Govern-ment Board and the Town Council. Many properties in Chapel Street and the surrounding area needed to be cleared, and references in the LSWR Minute Books report on progress with the authorities. The company acquired suitable land in March 1898 in Lower Brook Street for £750, intended for the erection of 14 cottages.

In 1900, attention was focused upon the need to widen the Chapel Street Bridge, a need exacerbated by the awkward road junction at this point. The west end of the new station would extend over the bridge and the Engineer recommended to the Board that the widening would best be carried out by placing a single span structure over the two roads, at their divergence. The Local Authority also took an interest in this, but their main concern seems to have been aesthetic, as a letter from the Basingstoke Town Clerk to the LSWR on 3rd November asks 'that the addition as well as the existing walls be faced with glazed white tiles.'

Despite having considered the estimates for white glazed bricks (£560), white tiles (£470) and Portland cement (£145), the company deferred a decision. Eventually, in May 1902, it was decided that white tiles, up to five feet above pavement level were to be provided at a much reduced cost of £30. At the same time, the LSWR agreed to pay £16-15s per annum to meet the expense of lighting the roadways disturbed by the new work.

Plans for the new Station buildings were first submitted to the Directors in July 1901, showing an estimated cost of £36,500. This had previously been reduced, for an unspecified reason, from £37,500. Final drawings and specifications were reported as ready at the Engineering Committee meeting on 21st January 1903. In anticipation of this, Messrs. Perry & Co. had, in fact, already offered to carry out the work. However, the LSWR invited tenders, and the contract was eventually awarded to Messrs. Kirk & Randall on 1st April 1903. This was formally signed on 20th April. Interestingly, this was one of very few contracts that this firm undertook in the South.

A reporter from *the Hants & Berks Gazette* visited the scene of activity in March 1903, escorted by the Assistant Engineer, Mr. Fisher, and wrote as follows:

'Some time in the year 1905, probably early in the year, people going up Station Hill will be faced by an imposing block of new buildings some 300 feet wide constructed of red brick with Portland type dressings and picturesque tiled roofs. Those buildings will form the new South Western Railway Station, The contract for the erection of which has just been undertaken by Messrs. Kirk and Randall of Woolwich. The buildings and works have been designed by Mr Jacomb Hood the Company's Chief Engineer, and will be carried out

Opposite page, top - The finishing touches to the new station building are apparent in this view. In the background adjacent to the new work is the station master's house. Of note is the magnificent telegraph pole dominating the front of the building and wires feeding into the telegraphic office can clearly be seen. Beyond the telegraph pole jutting out is the booking hall, described at the time as a "splendid chamber". It extended upwards to the roof of the building being twice the height of the waiting rooms and other offices.

Bottom - Ground floor accommodation included booking hall, parcels office, telegraph office, stores and at platform level, the waiting rooms, refreshment rooms and kitchens (see ground plan on page 28). Electric powered lifts were installed to ease transport of passenger luggage. The stationmaster, Mr Prince, now had jurisdiction from Worting Junction to Barton Mill signal boxes and responsibility for 130 men, including 22 signalmen, 14 goods clerks, 21 shunters, 6 parcel porters, 9 guards, 3 station inspectors, 3 ticket collectors and 8 porters. Both 'The Railway Magazine'.

A closer view of the station entrance with the awning under construction. The booking hall is to the right. The whole of the building is heated by steam with radiators instead of the usual open fireplaces. It was stated at the time that this was the first time the LSWR had installed such a system on it's network. An electrical generator supplied power to the station which in turn provided the steam heating. Later in November 1913, the LSWR Engineer recommended the abolition of the plant with the Town Council supplying lighting and power at a cost saving of £260 pa. A report dated 17th December 1914 confirms this had taken place under a ten year agreement.   Photo 'The Railway Magazine'

under the supervision of Mr. Szlumper, the District Engineer and his Assistant, Mr. A.J. Fisher of Basingstoke.

'Arrangements will of course have to be made for the Company's traffic. Subject to this, execution of the work will proceed as rapidly as possible, but it is expected that it will not be completed for at least eighteen months.

'In order to make room for the new lines of railway that are to be laid in accordance with the scheme of widening now in process of development, the existing station buildings on the down side will be demolished and the new buildings will be brought down to the gateway close to the Junction Inn and Messrs. Raynbird & Sons offices. The result of this will be that the ground floor of the new station will be below the level of the platform. Passengers will enter the station through a large booking hall with two lobbies and will pass through a spacious subway to be connected by corridor with the existing subway which will be extended to the face of the new buildings. The main subway will be lined with white glazed bricks. It will be eighteen feet wide and will be divided by a barrier, on one side of which passengers will pass, the other side being intended for luggage. Passengers will ascend to any of the three platforms by a flight of stairs, at the top of which there will be ornamental iron gates. Luggage will be raised by lifts. The buildings on the ground floor will include parcels and telegraph stores and a parcels office which will be connected by a lift with other parcels office and a cloak room on the down platform above, where also will be found a general waiting room, two ladies waiting rooms, telegraph office for the use of the public and one for the use of the Company, station master's office, inspector's office, ticket collector's office, porter's room, store, accommodation for mail bags, and lumber room, together with all the other accommodation usually found at a first rate station.

Persons wishing to use the Subway to cross from Station Hill to South View will still continue to enjoy the use.

'At the top of the steps leading from the subway to the Down platform, provision has been made for a bookstall. To the west of this there will be a large separate block of buildings three storeys high for the Refreshment Department. The ground floor will be taken up with kitchen, stores, larders, wine cellars etc. Level with the down platform there will be a large refreshment bar and dining room, and the floor above will be devoted to the living rooms, bedrooms, bathrooms etc. for the refreshment staff.

'To the west of the refreshment rooms will be the new residence for the Station Master, the foundations of which are now being prepared. This will be the first part of the new station to be erected, and we understand the refreshment department will then be proceeded with. The Station Master's house will be a two-storey building with large bay window. It will include two good sized living rooms, about 16 feet by 14 feet, three or four bedrooms and will be fitted with all the latest improvements.

'The Down platform will be no less than one thousand feet long and will be stone paved. The existing Down platform will then form the central or island platform. The buildings now standing upon it will be demolished and in their place will be erected new waiting rooms, refreshment rooms, lock-up parcels office and accommodation for foot-warming apparatus. The Up platform will remain pretty much as it is now, except that the present waiting rooms will be taken away to make room for the new subway steps, lift etc. and the new waiting rooms will be built at the eastern end of the platform. Bookstalls will be built on all three platforms. They will not however project as do the existing ones, but will form part of the station building proper. Platform roofs will be erected, the Down platform one extending the entire length, the other two being some 500 feet.

'The whole of the station buildings will be heated with steam so that fireplaces and chimneys will be conspicuous by their absence. The only rooms enjoying the luxury of a fireplace and chimney will be the porter's room and the chamber for the heating apparatus.

'The question of lighting the station has yet to be decided. It does not seem probable that the Bas. Corporation will be early enough in the field with their long-talked of electric light to enable the Company to avail themselves of it; but it is almost certain that the lighting will be done by electricity.

The Goods Department

'This will be brought into use almost immediately. Hitherto the goods department has been carried on in the yard on the eastern side of the station

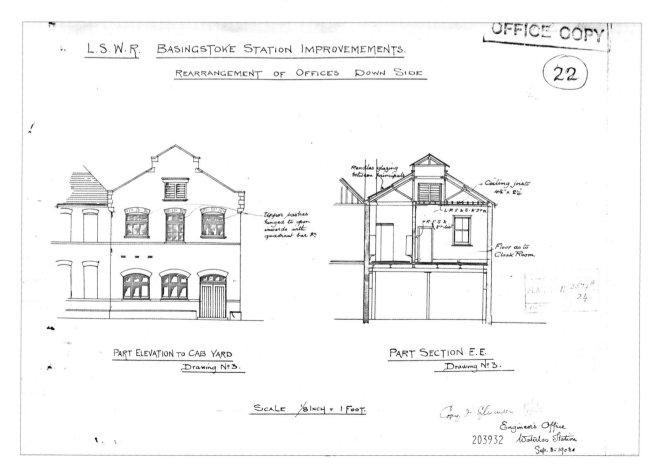

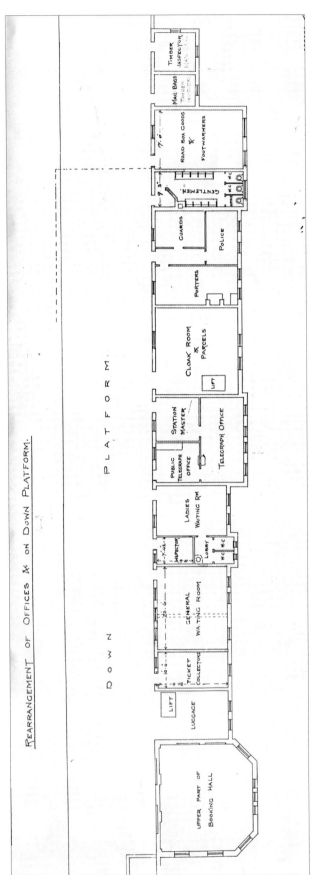

REARRANGEMENT OF OFFICES & ON DOWN PLATFORM.

PLATFORM

DOWN

UPPER PART OF BOOKING HALL

LIFT

LUGGAGE

TICKET COLLECTORS

GENERAL WAITING ROOM

LOBBY

INSPECTOR

LADIES WAITING RM

WC WC

PUBLIC TELEGRAPH OFFICE

STATION MASTER

TELEGRAPH OFFICE

CLOAK ROOM & PARCELS

LIFT

PORTERS

POLICE

GUARDS

GENTLEMEN

WC

ROAD BOX GOODS

FOOTWARMERS

MAIL BAGS

TIMBER INSPECTOR

with an approach from Bunnion Place. The new development necessitates the removal of the old goods office, the site of which will presently be occupied by additional pairs of metals. The new yard and offices have been constructed on the western side of the station, and the transfer of the staff and apparatus will be made in the course of the next week or two.

'This new accommodation for the goods department has been provided on a scale of considerable magnitude and outside London there are probably few if any stations on the Company's system which can boast of better or ampler accommodation in this respect. The impression one gets in going round the new yard and buildings is that an enormous quantity of goods traffic is expected to be dealt with here in the days to come.

'The yard is approached by a new road, the entrance to which is from Chapel Street immediately opposite Junction Road. There is an upward incline towards the yard which looks rather stiff for horses with loaded wagons, but Mr. Fisher remarked that the gradient was not so steep as it looks, being only 1 in 20, whereas the gradient of Station Hill is 1 in 12. The road up the incline is bounded on the left by a brick wall, on the other side of which are the Brewery premises and on the right, by a massive concrete wall, the height of which tapers off towards the top of the incline. The yard itself, which has been constructed with soil obtained from land alongside the light railway between the Worting and Winchester roads, has been properly gravelled. It comprises an area of between 4-5 acres and will afford room for 2-3 miles of additional sidings.

'The goods shed is a commodious structure nearly 200 feet long and 70 or 80 feet wide. Within we find two spacious platforms, beside each of which is a line of rails upon which some 20 wagons can be run into the shed. At each end of these lines are sliding doors. Upon the platforms stand four large cranes. On the approach side of the shed are five cart bays with sliding doors. The building has an iron trussed roof with skylight The offices are at the eastern end or the building. Immediately adjacent to the main shed is the ware-housemen's and checkers office, with windows commanding a view of the interior of the shed. Ample accommodation for the clerical staff has been provided. On the ground floor is a large office fitted with a counter for the public and plenty of cupboards, desks and pigeon holes for the clerks. Above it on the first floor is another commodious office some 20 feet square whose windows command a view of the station and the entire town of Basingstoke with the hills of Kempshott and Farleigh in the distance. There is also a Chief Clerk's office on the same floor and a lavatory on the landing. In the basement there is room for the storage of years of correspondence. It will thus be seen that the Company have made provision for a considerable future development of the Goods Department.

Moving inside the station, the commodious facilities are a major improvement on the Victorian station. The platforms left to right, are Down Local, Down Main, Up Main, Up Local. The Island platform was 32 feet wide and the accommodation consisted of a foot warmers room, urinal, general and ladies waiting room, parcels office, bookstall, refreshment room with cellar, staircase to subway, lift and "gentlemans court". Water supply to the station was provided by Basingstoke Corporation until 1930 when the SR Engineer recommended a well discovered on the company's property should be tapped which would save an estimated £244 pa. This appears to have been done as it was reported on 23rd July 1931 that pumps had been purchased and a plant installed.

'Farmers and stock-breeders who send supplies to Messrs. Raynbird & Sons (market and cattle dealers) who take them away, will be interested to learn that cattle will be loaded and unloaded on the eastern side of the station near the same spots as at present.

'Passing from the new goods shed to the opposite side of the line, we see in the process of erection the new engine shed which is being built by Sir J.T. Firbank with which will be connected storerooms, mess rooms and other accommodation for the men. The iron trussed roof is now being constructed and before many months have rolled by the building will doubtless be ready for use. It will accommodate nine engines whereas the old building which will presently be demolished, sheltered only two.

'On the northern side of it where Messrs. Tagart, Morgan & Coles timber yard formerly was, ground has been excavated for the construction of the turntable and for the accommodation of the stacks of coal that will be required for the supply of engines. Near

here will take place the entraining of horses and a way into this spot will be made from the Rising Sun.'

A bay platform on the down side was incorporated into the new facilities, to accommodate traffic of the recently-opened Basingstoke and Alton Light Railway. The original opening of this line had been delayed by the extensive engineering work in the area. The LSWR Directors had been informed on 30th July 1900 that the contractors for the light railway, Joseph Firbank (also involved in the widening contract to Worting Junction), had 'practically finished', but that the new line at the Basingstoke end was in use for the conveyance of chalk required for the enlargement of the station area and 'until this work was finished, the railway cannot be reported as ready for opening'. Sanction for this line had been granted by the BOT in late 1897, interestingly the first under the 1896 Light Railways Act.

Work commenced in July 1898 close to

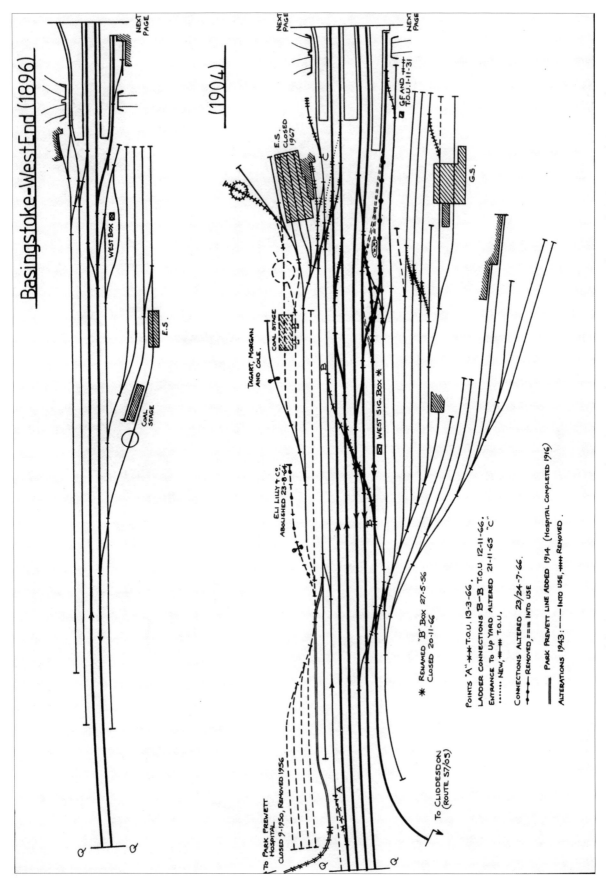

Basingstoke–West End (1896)

(1904)

From TRACK LAYOUT DIAGRAMS of the SOUTHERN RAILWAY and BR S.R. Section S7 NORTH HAMPSHIRE G A Pryer and A V Paul

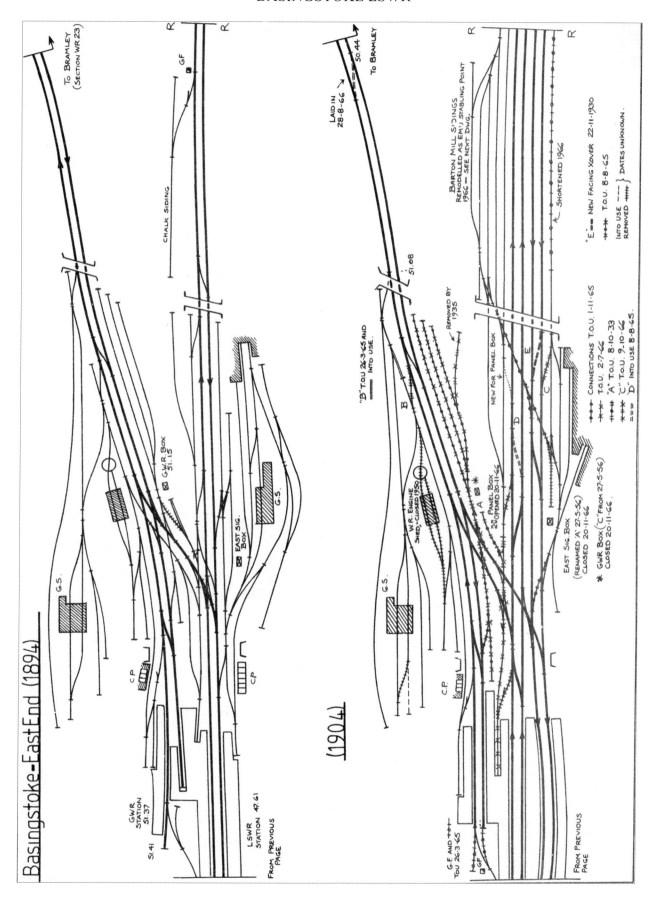

Basingstoke-East End (1894)

(1904)

Messrs. Thorneycroft's new Basingstoke works on the fringe of the town. Construction of the 12½ mile line was largely uneventful, and the branch eventually opened, following the afore-mentioned delay, on 1st June 1901. A modest service of three trains each way was initiated, with optimistic hopes for a steady growth in traffic. Alas, this never materialised, and services remained much the same throughout the railway's relatively short life. One interesting feature, which has recently come to light, was an original proposal for a flyover junction at Basingstoke, showing the branch joining the main line on the Up side instead of the Down, as built. The LSWR's obsession at the time with this type of arrangement was soon modified, presumably on grounds of cost.

Whilst the early sections of the rebuilding were under way, a very ambitious scheme was being floated which would, if realised, have greatly affected Basingstoke as a railway centre. Proposals for the highly-improbable Bristol, Bath and Southern Counties Railway were published in 1902, with a Bill to go before the Select Committee seeking powers to build a 73½ mile line from Bristol to Basingstoke via Trowbridge and Bulford, to join the LSWR at Overton. This scheme, similar to the earlier Basing and Bath proposals, was an attempt by Bristol businessmen to relieve their city of the Great Western monopoly, and the burden of traffic rates charged by that company. The project required a capital of £4,500,000, and went before the House of Commons Committee in June 1903. Despite assurances that the necessary sum could be raised, the Bill was rejected as not being in the public interest. Thus, Basingstoke was deprived of the opportunity to become an even more significant junction on the nation's railway map.

The GWR was not to be outshone by the large-scale improvements of its close neighbour and undertook some upgrading work on its own facilities early in 1903. The old Middle platform between the arrival and departure roads was removed, enabling the arrival (Down) road to be slewed over towards the Up, thus permitting the arrival platform to be considerably widened by some six to seven feet; this eliminated the long-standing constriction caused by the narrowness of the former arrangement. The *Hants & Berks Gazette* recorded on 14th February that the platform was also to be lengthened by approximately 200 feet: 'The present platform has been found too short for the long trains bringing the through coaches from the Birkenhead and Newcastle districts to Bournemouth and other stations and some of the travelling public on reaching Basingstoke have had to alight on the ballast'; the cost of the work was stated as 'about' £1,000.

By the end of 1904 the new locomotive department and goods facilities were in full use at Basingstoke. The passenger station was all but complete, with some minor fittings and refurbishment work outstanding. The importance of the improved interchange facilities for goods traffic is amplified by returns for the period, which show as many as 900 wagon transfers between the LSWR and the GWR per week. The *Railway Magazine* described the accommodation in April 1905:

'Before the improvements were effected, the tranship work used to be dealt with in the old Great Western shed, but a new and commodious goods depot has been laid out at the West end of the new station, and thither the traffic from the north is now brought to be re-marshalled before being sent out again on its travels.

'There are also five bays and two stages for accommodating the local traffic to Basingstoke, and when it is mentioned that such large firms as Wallace and Steven's, Dowson's, and Thorneycroft's steam waggons (a special siding) have their habitat there, it will be recognised that this part of the work also is of considerable importance.

'While the goods warehouse is bounded on the north by the tranship sidings, and on the south by the sidings which serve the town, the east or terminal end forms the boundary wall for the goods clerks' offices, where fourteen men are employed.

'Close adjoining is the tank house, and under the tank itself is a mess room with accommodation for the carriage repairing staff. The old goods shed at the London end of the Station is now used only for the cattle pens, which it was deemed more convenient to leave unmoved on account of the proximity of the pens to the cattle market.'

During the latter part of the reconstruction, which included the installation of pneumatic signalling at Basingstoke – see the concluding article in a later

Opposite bottom - *A postcard view taken shortly after the rebuilt station was completed, showing the down bay platform complete with van. This was known as the Alton Bay and continued to be referred to as such for many years after closure of the light railway. The two sets of girders seen here support the bridging of the awkward road junction at this point. The widening entailed the extension of two underbridges at the junction of Chapel Street and Vyne Road. This was carried out by Messrs Aird as part of the widening contract but, with the additional increase of 5 shillings per cubic yard of concrete and 2 / 6d per cubic yard of brickwork. It was apparently necessary to undertake strengthening work in 1930 as it was reported on 26th June that steelwork was purchased from Messrs Horsehay & Co. for £189-11-8d for this purpose.*

Photo Authors Collection

Above - *A view of the station looking east. The only part of the Victorian station remaining is visible here on platform 4 the original up platform. Part of the earlier canopy, supported on cast iron columns with thistle-like heads, can be discerned. They were similar to those on the former down platform, swept away in the reconstruction. The boundary wall at the "country end" of the up platform and part of the building structure at the top of the subway stairs are also part of the original station. The down west end platform canopy was extended by 140 feet in January 1943.*

S.W. Ry. Station, Basingstoke. 3.

T.H.
B.

The down west goods yard required around 200,000 cubic yards of chalk to form the required embankment for the extension. It was reported on 16th October 1900 that the formation had been completed and that the walls of the goods shed and offices were well in hand. The entrance to the yard was off Chapel Street, framed by gates some 24 feet 2 inches between the pillars. This entrance required land to be purchased from Messrs May & Co for widening the old approach to the yard, and unspecified terms were agreed in February 1902. In 1946 a new covered stage at the west end of the goods shed was provided. It was noted that the shed was provided with three cranes of unstated capacity. An earlier note, in the Minute Books for February 1901, records these cranes as being supplied by Messrs Stothert & Pitt for £200. The goods shed office accommodation was improved in 1915 at a cost of £18 for the use of the cartage clerk. It had earlier been agreed to provide telephone communication in April 1898 at a cost of £8 pa. Further improvements were made, when it was found that the lighting of the yard and sidings was wanting and two extra lamps were provided in 1917 at a cost of £35. Various other accommodation provision were approved in the 1920's for Shell Mex Ltd and the Anglo-American Oil Co. A stores and mess room for female staff, adjacent to the goods shed, was provided in 1943 at a cost of £467.

'Southern Way', Major Pringle of the BOT was a periodic visitor. In his report following the inspection of 26th January 1906, Pringle commented:

'The extensive alterations in the station yard as regards passenger accommodation and working have been completed but I did not make an inspection of these new Works.'

On 16th March 1907 the Board of Trade were informed that all the new works, including the signalling arrangements, were ready for inspection. Major Pringle arrived again on 5th May and found very little to comment on considering the extent of the transformation at the station.

His attention was focused on the two extended underbridges, which were tested for deflections under the usual engine load. His comment seems a little guarded, stating that the new steel spans and supports have 'apparently sufficient theoretical strength'. Favourable remarks concerning the general standard of the new structures prefixed the formal approval note at the foot of the report.

FURTHER MINOR IMPROVEMENTS

Following the opening of the new LSWR station, the GWR found it necessary to write in early 1907 regarding the control of access between the two stations. In April, an agreement was reached whereby the GWR was to erect gates and 'unclimbable' fencing between the two platforms. The keys to the gates were to be held by the LSWR station master, and responsibility for maintenance would rest with the GWR. The latter company would pay the LSWR 2s 6d per annum for 'use of the access'.

It would seem that some difficulty of access also arose with the hinged gates controlling the stairways within the new station, as the LSWR approved their replacement on 5th April 1905 with 'collapsible' gates. These were supplied by the Bostwick Gate Company at an approximate cost of £40. Improvements in the facilities for the ticket collectors was forthcoming in February 1912, when shelters were provided on each

Rail access to Messrs Thornycrofts was provided by a siding off the light railway on a 330 feet radius curve. It was in use from about the opening of the Alton line. A plan dated 1930 shows the siding then fanned out into three roads with a back siding, together serving engine and boiler houses and workshops. The key to the gates across this private siding were kept in Basingstoke West signal box. In this view an 0-4-4T deals with some wagon transfers in LSWR days.

of the three platform areas, at an estimated cost of £45.

The subject of cartage arrangements came before the LSWR Traffic Committee in May 1913, when a proposal that the company should undertake its own provision, thereby saving £361 p.a. was considered. However, for reasons unrecorded, this was not proceeded with. The subject came up again in October 1915, being precipitated by the resignation of the company's agent Mr. Webb. This time, the LSWR decided to undertake the work, and ordered 6 single horse trolleys at an estimated cost of £282 and in March 1916, 2 single horse vans for parcels at an estimated cost of £95. The service would certainly seem to have been remunerative. For example, in 1924 the annual tonnage handled was 2,645, formed of some 2,847 loads.

A SPATE OF ACCIDENTS AND INCIDENTS

The period 1904 to 1919 played host to a series of unfortunate events, unparalleled throughout the station's history. Some of these were of a minor nature. For example, irregularities in working which, although undesirable, did not cause damage to persons or equipment. The first accident of the period, however, did result in death, and was described in the *Hampshire Chronicle* on 14th May 1904:

'Another fatality, this time at Basingstoke occurred on Thursday evening. The unfortunate victim was a shunter named Edward Compton (49). The accident took place at 6.35 pm, the deceased being engaged in shunting some wagons from the Great Western into the No. 3 road. He was walking along in the six foot way between the Up and Down main lines,

the Up line being between him and the wagons he was in charge of. The Up Weymouth express approached him, and noticing it coming he appears to have attempted to cross the line in front of the express towards the wagons he was shunting. Unfortunately he was not able to get clear in time and was struck by the engine. The express was travelling at 40 mph at the time and the man's body was carried 150 yards to just beyond Reading Road Bridge. The terribly mangled body was extricated and taken to the mortuary'.

On 12th May 1912, during a major thunderstorm, Steventon Signal Box was totally destroyed by fire. The wooden structure was subsequently repaired, at an estimated cost of £100. The cause of the fire was believed to have been a bolt of lightening fusing the electrical apparatus.

A derailment occurred on 28th March 1913, when the 2.20pm Basingstoke to Salisbury goods was traversing points at the west end of the station. The engine began slipping badly in maneuvering the heavy train, then derailed, blocking both down lines. The condition of the track at this point was later blamed for the incident.

No doubt the exigencies of war contributed to many of the incidents and adversities occurring in that turbulent period. With railway staff working long hours, the inevitable momentary lapses of concentration surfaced from time to time:

6th July 1914 - 11.00 am Bournemouth West to Waterloo train overran Worting Junction Up home signal by 100 yards. Driver Eve cautioned.

26th December 1914 - 10.30 am Waterloo to Southampton train ran through Basingstoke East Down home signal by 200 yds. Driver Stone cautioned.

6th February 1917 - Driver Stevens run over and killed by an engine at No. 2 siding in West Yard carriage sidings.

13th May 1917 - At 11.15 am, engine working 9.40 am Southampton to Waterloo train derailed at points leading from Up local line to Up siding. Porter and Signalman at fault.

12th October 1917 - An empty stock train being shunted collided sideways with a stationary passenger train. One passenger slightly injured.

29th May 1918 - Driver Hughes killed whilst oiling the inside motion of his engine whilst at coal stage. A cleaner had moved the engine. The cleaner and fireman were severely criticised at the inquest.

28th October 1919 - At 3.27 am, the 1.15 am goods from Southampton to Nine Elms broke a tyre on a tender wheel at Worting Junction Signal Box. Caused by defective workmanship.

22nd March 1920 - With the assistance of the police. Head Porter W Puddocke apprehended two soldiers who were responsible for the theft of a mailbag from the station.

Opposite, top - Mr Prince with some of his staff pose on the station forecourt. He must have been quite proud of his new charge, which was one of the most modern stations in Britain at the time. By 1917 Prince had risen to high office, as station superintendent at Waterloo.

Opposite, bottom - The splendid new station buildings shortly after being fully commissioned. In the foreground is the entrance to the booking office, and the awning is now complete. The clock turret above the booking office is, of course, facing the town. It was illuminated at night.

Above - The few buildings in close proximity to escape demolition during the enlargement are seen here. None of these survive today of course, obliterated in the wholesale reconstruction (some would say destruction) of the town centre in the 1960's.

WITH THANKS TO COLIN CHIVERS FOR HIS ASSISTANCE WITH PHOTOGRAPHS

REAL ATMOSPHERE

ENGINE ARRANGEMENTS

If you have already glanced at the inside covers, you will have noticed an advert for one of our new titles 'George Heiron's Southern Collection'. In the course of sourcing the material for this book we were also able to obtain a very few photographs of Victoria and shown here.

Was it really only a few short years between engines as seen here, in apparent perfect external condition and the filthy examples that saw out the end of steam in 1967? 34100 'Appledore' depicts all that was best at Stewarts Lane, and whilst recorded by the camera in profile, the front portion alone comes very close to being mistaken for a 'Britannia'. The reasons for which are well known relative to the designs of Ron Jarvis in the 1950s. No dates unfortunately, but it is likely it was 1961, possibly the very last steam hauled 'Golden Arrow. 34100 had been allocated to Ramsgate from new and spent the next ten years here and at Stewarts Lane. Rebuilt in August / September 1960, it returned to Stewarts Lane for a short time before moving to Brighton and eventually Salisbury. It was withdrawn after the last steam workings in July 1967 and did not survive into preservation.

Opposite is Victoria in peacetime, obviously so perhaps, but it makes an interesting comparison with the spread at the start of this issue. George had a knack of capturing not just the train, but the general scene as well. Look at the bottom view and more and more detail emerges with each viewing. There are several views of the concourse at Waterloo in the aforementioned book as well.

George Heiron / The Transport Treasury.

Previous pages - Rod Hoyle of course. 73067 and the brazier are just inside the shed door at Salisbury, as is the 'Engine Arrangements' board shown in the inset. Both were photographed in the winter of 1966/67. By this time, of course, Salisbury steam duties had diminished somewhat, hence the limited number of entries shown. Opposite another pair of 'standards' are recorded, this time outside Basingstoke shed.

34100 'Appledore' again, now climbing away from Platform 8 at Victoria a few moments after 11.00 am. Arrival at Dover was at 12.37 pm ready for a 1.05 pm sailing. This crossing took 1 hr and 20 minutes, with the Paris train arriving at Gare de Nord at 6.10 pm. A total of 7hrs 10 minutes for a journey, now possible in little over 3hrs by more modern rail traction. Steam workings ended on 11th June 1961 whilst there was also a gradual reduction in the compliment of Pullman vehicles. The service, by now electric hauled, finally ended on 30th September 1972.

George Heiron / The Transport Treasury

But, and bearing in mind the location of the view, this leads us very nicely into a sequel overleaf to the article in 'SW3' "Victoria 9th December 1949 - a sad mistake"…………

VICTORIA, DECEMBER 1949 - Revisited

(Additional information from 'SW3')

Following the article that appeared in the Spring issue of *SOUTHERN WAY* (Issue No 3), we were contacted by Chris Duffell who sent the attached newspaper cutting. He comments, "The article reminded me that I had a newspaper cutting from the time of the accident. As I was only eight and a bit years old, I did not think of keeping the reference, little realising that 58+ years later I would be sending it to someone! Our regular paper was the *NEWS CHRONICLE*, so I assume it comes from that paper, dated 10th December. I lived in south London at the time, quite near West Norwood from where Mr Sydney, quoted in the cutting, came. It is interesting to read that he and others thought the power to the third rail was still on. Maybe that reflected wartime experiences when, I believe, people were evacuated from trains with the power still on. One photograph in the cutting does show a bit of the accident and damage to the caches. With everything sorted by early morning the next day, one cannot help wondering for how long the station would be closed these days....."

The newspaper report stated as follows, **"Golden Arrow in Collision. Passengers are led to safety by torches.** "Golden Arrow", the famous boat train bringing passengers from Paris, was in a threefold rail crash at the approaches to Victoria Station, London, last night. First the cream-and-brown luxury train scraped alongside a 100-ton engine which was to draw the Arrow's empty coaches out of the station. The 100-tonner tilted over and raked the windows and woodwork

of the outgoing 6.40 train to West Croydon. Seven of the passengers on the Croydon train and the engine's crew of two were slightly hurt or suffered shock. They were treated in hospital

"Coaches scarred - Nobody on the Golden Arrow train was injured, but the engine was dented and the first five coaches scarred. Pieces of wood and glass fell on the track. The 95 passengers from Paris were led by railway officials, police and fireman - all carrying torches - over an electrified line on to the platform. The second portion of the Golden Arrow was stopped at Herne Hill and passengers were taken on by bus. Another express, the Thanet Belle, was held up at Herne Hill, and passengers were taken on to Victoria in a fleet of buses. Trains on the services from Victoria which serves the North Kent area were diverted to Blackfriars.

"The Casualties - Those taken to hospital were Driver Patrick Sheehan and Fireman Albert Turner, of Stewarts Lane Depot, who were on the derailed engine: Oliver Marshall (17), of Hobart Street, SW11, Leopold Telesnicki (39) and Benedict Draczynski (47), both of Mowbray Street SE19, Joan Leman (17) of Trollope Street SW8, Mrs Fitt (41) of Mowbray Road, Upper Norwood, John William Howills of Strathevan Road SW1, and Guard Denny of the Victoria Depot. Passengers in the damaged portion of the electric train were kept waiting half an hour in darkened compartments before being allowed to walk the 400 yards back to the platform.

"Woman "-scared" - Mr W A Sydney of West Norwood, told me, "It was pitch dark and, although some railwaymen tried to light our way with oil lamps, many of us felt the whole proceedings were rather dangerous. Elderly people found it difficult to climb down out of the train, and the women were scared of walking through the darkness so close to the live rails."

(From other sources the train formations have also come to light. 'The 'Golden Arrow' make up being, locomotive 34084, PMV Baggage Van No 1293, 'Conflat' 39636, Pillman No 99, Pullman No 294, 'Malaga', 'Onyx', 'Zenobia', The Trianon Bar', Chloria' and 'Floria'. The eight car EMU (two four car sets) in order from the leading vehicle were set No 4594 (9822-9301-11456-8223) and set No 4546 (8884, 9749, 10223, 8718).

Separate reports refer to an amount of pilfering taking place from the Pullman vehicles, which included most of the table lamps. The Ministry of Transport report, from which much of the information in the original article was drawn, was published on 15th March 1950.

With grateful thanks also to Bob Radcliffe for additional contributions on this subject.

"THE *SWAYING* FOOTPLATE"

Part 2 of former Southern Railwayman Norman Denty's experience in the Traffic and Locomotive departments.

(Continuing the story from Southern Way No 2. Norman is now with the loco department as a young fireman at Bournemouth in WW2.)

Starting at Bournemouth in the autumn of 1943, I was initially put onto the Poole Quay shunter. The first job on early turn was to prepare a 'B4' and run the five miles light to Poole Yard. Here we collected perhaps five or more wagons and two shunters, before trundling off in the reverse direction to the Quayside. One of the shunters would ride with us at the front and the other with the guard, their purpose being to stop road traffic running into the train as we negotiated various cross-roads and T-junctions, whilst running in what was, in effect, a half circle to reach our destination.

At one point the railway ran along the right hand side of West Quay Road and it was here that we would stop at the workman's café. The driver, guard and shunters would all pile in for refreshment, whilst vans and lorries would arrive and park behind the train, their drivers joining us in the café.

My lodgings at Bournemouth were reasonable, although every day the landlady would give me plain cheese sandwiches, not a particular favourite. However toasted cheese sandwiches were more edible and of course the obvious solution was courtesy of the firebox. Later, when in another gang, we arrived one day at Poole yard with a 'K10' on a local goods. During our break my driver was frying some chops, again on the shovel and resting on the fire hole ring. Unfortunately it was just at this point that the shunter came up and asked if we could move just a few yards further up. My driver dutifully obliged, but completely forgot about his lunch with the inevitable consequences. He had no one to blame but himself. I remember the sky on that autumn day was pure blue, although the colour was nothing compared to the language on the footplate.

For crews at Bournemouth, the number of passenger workings greatly exceeded the number of freight workings, although one goods turn I did look forward to was a down Feltham service which we were booked to take over at Eastleigh. After signing on, it was a case of look at the notice board, to check there was nothing different applicable to the turn. Assuming not, we would ride on the cushions as far as Eastleigh ready to take over the train.

The engine on the trains was usually a WD 2-8-0. Contrary to what others have said, I found the class to be excellent, free steaming with plenty of space in the cab. At times and for various reasons there was a shortage of Bournemouth drivers, so more than once I travelled to Eastleigh on my own ready to work the train through to its destination at Poole yard, with an Eastleigh driver on overtime. If these engines though did have one fault, it was the drawbar between the engine and tender. Up to about 35 mph it was fine, but exceed 40 and the whole thing would start to vibrate shaking the life out of us on the footplate. We might have 50, 60 or more wagons behind the tender and as we also had to keep clear of passenger trains, especially after Southampton, we had to motor on.

Arrival at Poole saw us propel the train into the yard and then run tender first back to Bournemouth.

Bournemouth crew, Driver T Watts and Fireman Ron Stoneman on No 850 in wartime black and with the cabside window plated over. Bournemouth West, 1944.

Here it was my job to clean out the smokebox and firebox, whilst, if it was an Eastleigh man was working the turn, it was now his opportunity to return home on the cushions.

It was whilst at Bournemouth that I experienced for the first time working on one of the former Brighton tank engines, that had been rebuilt as tender engines in the form of the 'N15X' class. By now I was also on occasional passenger work, my driver and I waiting at Bournemouth Central to relieve a set of Nine Elms men on a train from Waterloo. Our job was to take the loco and first six coaches on to their final destination at Weymouth. At this time the rebuilt 'N15X' engines were split between Nine Elms, Basingstoke, whilst some were on loan to the GWR. Hence they could also be found on trains to and from Oxford.

We had No 2333 'Remembrance', the fact that I had worked on Brighton engines previously, although not an 'N15X', meaning I had no fear of what was to come. How wrong I was going to be.

Leaving Bournemouth there is a slight rise to the first station at Branksome, although already I had noticed that the cab was moving one way and the firebox the other. Also, there was a noticeable hole in the wooden floor of the cab immediately behind the rear driving wheel on the fireman's side. Not a pretty sight as the flanges could be seen to wobble over the various crossovers and round the curves. This was a sight I was unaccustomed to, having also had no experience of the 'Q1' design at this time. The whole experience was definitely off-putting, but working on the basis that if I ignored it, it might go away, I continued shovelling coal into what seemed to be an ever hungry firebox, as well as just managing to make sure the water level remained

where it should be in the boiler. Even so the injector was on almost continually and I was shovelling likewise. Literally then, 'The Swaying Footplate'.

Somehow we made it to Weymouth, helped by the fact that it is downhill for the last few miles. We were booked to take the engine and coaches back to Bournemouth, at which station a further six coaches would be added, meaning a 12 coach load for the run to Waterloo.

Preparing the engine for its return run, the reason for our troubles immediately became apparent as I was cleaning the ashes from the smokebox. Two or three tubes were leaking badly. There was no way this engine was going to make it back to Waterloo, whilst we would need help with just six coaches, on leaving Weymouth and also later on Parkstone bank. My driver contacted the running foreman at Bournemouth to tell him the news, after which somehow, we made it back to Bournemouth with the aid of the Poole station pilot, an 'M7', which took a break from shunting the station yard to give us a much needed shove from behind. At Bournemouth Central I was somewhat relieved to uncouple and take the engine onto the disposal pits, this being one duty where the engine would be dealt with by a disposal crew. I never saw No 2333 again. To my mind these rebuilds were never a patch on the Urie rebuilds of the Drummond 4-6-0s although my favourite locos still have to be the Brighton 'Atlantics'.

As I moved up the links I knew I would soon become acquainted with the 'Nelsons'. This first came about with the afternoon '2 to 10' or sometimes '4 to12' duties. On these turns we took a member of the class for a passenger working on the short section between Bournemouth Central and Bournemouth West. The London trains were all 12 coaches at this time and we

The footplate of a 'K10' with Driver Ted Vigor (right) and Fireman Ron Stoneham, this time at Brockenhurst in 1945. It was on an engine of this type and with Ted driving, that Norman experienced being shot at whilst working a train load of petrol. Ron and Norman also shared lodgings for a while. Ron was a keen photographer even managing to obtain a limited amount of film at this time. They likewise became close friends.

would take half of these on, the other half heading to Weymouth as described earlier. We would then return light to Bournemouth Central and prepare the engine to take the whole train back to Waterloo later on. Before this, though, it was the short run to the 'West' already mentioned, then propel the six coaches up the bank to the carriage sidings. Arriving back at the depot, servicing could take some time. I recall one occasion when cleaning out the smokebox alone took me an hour, although the job I detested most was filling up the sandboxes. I also had the task of shovelling the coal forward in the tender.

After this it was turn the loco and back to Bournemouth West, to take, usually, the same six coaches as far as 'Central'. Another Bournemouth crew, but in the top-link, would continue with the combined portions from Bournemouth West and Weymouth. They would also receive mileage for this working, the round trip being 232 miles. This was definitely the link to be in, but it took a few years for a fireman to reach and even longer for a driver.

My first proper working on a 'Nelson' proper was on another Bournemouth to Weymouth and return duty, also a service that started and finished at Waterloo. It was a hot day and I made the mistake of nipping over the low wall at Weymouth loco to the local "Strongs" public house for a pint of rough cider. Leaving Weymouth I was definitely suffering from the effects of a light head, although having to fire that 10' 6" firebox up the gradient to Bincombe Tunnell meant that any effects had been disposed of by the time Dorchester was reached. At Dorchester there was the peculiar arrangement whereby up trains would stop on the guard waving his red flag and then reverse, again under the instructions of the guard's flags, into the platform. Incidentally that was the first and also the last time, I ever tried rough cider – I have been a 'mild' man ever since.

One occasion when we were lucky was with a petrol special from the wartime fuel dump at West Moors, travelling via Ringwood on a train destined for Southampton Docks. My driver was Ted Vigor and we had a 'K10' 4-4-0. We had just passed through Ringwood and were climbing the gradients through the forest when there was a sound totally different from that made by the engine. Ted and I both looked at each blankly for an instance before turning to look back down the train. There we both saw the same thing, an enemy aircraft fast disappearing. What we had both heard of coursewas his attempt at machine gunning us. Bearing in mind our cargo, we were indeed lucky that he had not been on target. Fortunately the rest of the trip was completed without incident.

Mention earlier of SR locomotives on loan reminds me that for a while, the LMS 'S & D' engines

were, for some reason, stabled at Bournemouth Central. There was also a Bournemouth Central cleaner promoted to Fireman, who regularly worked to Bath Green Park and back on an LMS '2P'. This working seemed to pass me quite often when I was waiting at Poole. One day I was also 'on loan to the LMS', the engine a '4F', which we took light to Poole and then onto a local freight, destined eventually for Evercreech Junction. Our first stop after Poole was Bailey Gate, where we shunted the yard before moving on to Blandford. Here we banged a few more trucks about before waiting for a passenger service to arrive from Bath. Now we changed footplates and I was able to have my first experience of a 'Black 5'. Great locomotives too.

Promotion found me in the "local goods and passenger link", with a regular driver, Bob Adams. One particular day we had an 'L12' on an afternoon homeward bound workman's train from Wareham. The job appeared to be all the sweeter, as waiting on the platform at Wareham was my girl friend at the time, who worked at a nearby factory. She came up to the engine, whilst my mate, knowing that she lived at Hamworthy Junction, invited her to ride with us on the footplate. We were now all stations to Bournemouth and to liven up proceedings a bit I invited her to have a go with the shovel. She was rather good, although perhaps a bit enthusiastic, as it was not long before coal – and shovel, were in the firebox. Bob was a placid man, he never said a word.

Somehow I managed to feed the fire just with my hands for the remainder of the journey, including having enough in the box to tackle Parkstone Bank. The most difficult bit, though, was at Bournemouth shed, as we had to hand in a complete set of tools to the storeman at the end of the duty. Luckily I was able to find an old, although somewhat battered shovel amongst the piles of debris in the shed. Even though the storeman gave me a quizzical look, it saved a lot of embarrassing questions. Later, the same girl friend told me she had also been seen by the signalman getting off the engine at Hamworthy Junction. She had been chastised by him in no uncertain manner. That signalman was her father!

The war years brought many different types of train movement, in lieu of what had been pre-war holiday traffic. These included troop, prisoner of war, munitions, stores and other types of working. We also dealt with Ambulance trains, lengthy workings, often with 15 or 16 bogie vehicles behind the tender. One of these saw me with a top-link passenger driver on an 'S15', which we took tender first, light engine, from Bournemouth to Blandford, there to take over the train from an LMS engine and crew. We never knew where these services started from, it was probably best not to ask too many questions. All we knew was the eventual there were four rooms, one of which was a slate-floored scullery/kitchen with a copper, kitchen range and pump for well water, discharging over a slopstone. There were two sitting rooms. That at the front was quite small, the other at the rear was larger, but had a cast iron column passing through its centre to support the workshop floor above. These columns were repeated throughout the ground floor of the workshop area. The last room was used as an office, with doors into the residential area and into the workshop. The office was equipped with a telephone, one of the first to be installed in the town. An indoor water closet had been installed, with drainage to a pair of cesspits a short distance outside. But the water for flushing had to be supplied from a bucket. Electric lighting, by carbon filament lamp bulbs, was available in the house, but only on the rare occasions when the plant in the workshop was running. The electricity was generated by a dynamo, belt-driven by the oil engine providing the power to the workshop. My father and siblings occasionally were allowed to stay up to witness this rare phenomenon employing carbon filament lamp bulbs, a magic change from the normal light from oil lamps and candles. Contemporary photographs show oil paintings on the walls and an old Georgian bureau, all of which I still have in my own home some 100 years later.

WORKPLACES

a. - Water Mills:-

Alcester, Warwicks. - Moor Hall Farm.
Alresford, Hants.
Atherstone, Warwicks. - Sheepy Mill
Bishop's Waltham, Hants.
Bordon, Hants. - Headley Mill - F. Ellis & Sons.
Botley, Hants.
Cardiff, - Henry Latham.

Cardiff, - Llandaff Mill - Marquess of Bute.
Cardiff, - Tregasky Mill.
Chichester, Sussex - Ham Farm - William Aylwin.
East Meon, Hants - Frogmore Mill - Benjamin Aylwin
Eversley, Hants. - 'New Mill' (300 years old!)
Fareham, Hants. - Fareham Steam Mills - Easeman.
Fareham, Hants. - Edney Bros.
Fareham, Hants. - Peel Common (Windmill).
Fittleworth, Sussex.
Guernsey, C.I. - Hocarts Mill (Haut Cart?) Windmill.
Hambledon, Hants. - Lord Hambledon.
Heathfield, Sussex. - Cross-in-Hand Mill.
Heathfield, Sussex. - Neve Bros.
Heathfield, Sussex. - Ticehurst Mill.
Henley-on-Thames. - Hambledon Mill - Barnett & Sons.
Iping, Sussex. - Evered.
Kingsclere, Hants. - Printing Works & Mansion - Lord Portal.
Midhurst, Sussex. - Baldwin Mill - Gwillam.
Midhurst, Sussex. - Queen Elizabeth Mill.
Overton, Hants. - Quidhampton Paper Mills - Lord Portal
Petersfield, Hants. - Hurst Mill - Whitman.
Petworth, Sussex. - Coultershaw Mill - Lord Leconfield - Gwillam, father & son.
Reading, Berks. - Calcot Mill - Thos: J. Dewe
Ringwood, Hants. - G. E. Bartlett.
Romsey, Hants. - Middlebridge Mill.
Romsey, Hants. - Sutton's Mill.
Romsey, Hants. - Town Mills.
Salisbury, Wilts. - John V. Armitage.
Salisbury, Wilts. - Frank Snelgar.
Salisbury, Wilts. - Henry Job Sutton's Mill.
St. Leonards, Sussex - Draper.
Sheet, Hants. - Sheet Bridge Mill - F. Ellis & Sons.
Sittingbourne, Kent - Carta Carna Biscuit Works - F. C.

Not to be of the best quality but included for interest's sake. The rural nature of the approach to Romsey station is exemplified in this view, probably taken a century ago. The diagonal fencing was an LSWR feature seen at a number of locations.

The original name for the signal box at Romsey, the junction being between the original 1847 route from Eastleigh (Bishopstoke) and the later 1865 line from Redbridge. The Adams 4-4-0 may well be on a Portsmouth - Salisbury working, via Eastleigh.   *All photographs - Paul Cooper collection*

Lowe & Sons.
Sittingbourne, Kent - J. Draper & Sons' Mill
Soberton, Hants. - St. Clair's Farm - C. House & Sons.
Tichfield, Hants. - Co-op Mill.
Totton, Hants -
Whitchurch, Hants. - Town Mills.
Wickham, Hants. - 'Chesapeake' Mill - Wm: Godrich.
Winchester, Hants. - Co-op Mill.

b. - 1907-1931 - Machinery made at Romsey for:-
Bathampton, Somerset - Harbutts Plasticine.
Devon Mushrooms.
Eastleigh, Hants. - Pirelli Tyre & Rubber.
Guernsey, Channel Islands - Engineers.
Hythe, Hants. - British Power Boat Company.
Leicester - Soar Lane Works - Evans Mills.
Romsey, Hants. - Tomato Nurseries.
Romsey, Hants. - Jam Factory - Hattatt & Son.
Romsey, Hants. - Stonemasons - Grace & Sons.
Romsey, Hants. - Test Valley Iron Works.

Rotherham, Yorks. - Habershon Steels.
Southampton, Hants - Transport Dept.
War Office/Ministry of Munitions Contracts during WW1.
Whimple, Somerset. - Whiteway's Cider.

MACHINERY PRODUCED AT SALISBURY AND / OR ROMSEY

a. - Milling Plant
Bar Wrapper
Bean & Pea Washer
Centrifugals - for flour dressing
Composite Millstones
Grain Conditioner
Gravel washer
Man Lift - 'Paternoster' type
Mill Bills - replaceable bits, for dressing millstones
Oats Blancher
Plansifter
Portable Sifter

A superb photograph of 'T3' No 568 in the up sidings at Romsey, with what is described as a Salisbury to Eastleigh working. Whilst the engine is certainly clean, it is far from pristine, contradicting preconceptions of the Edwardian era. Although built as late as 1893, the influx of Drummond types saw the 'T3' class moved further westwards and all 20 were reported as in the Devon / Cornwall area by the end of 1906. The starting signals confirm the importance of the original route to Bishopstoke, being considered of greater importance compared with that to Redbridge.

housed the cooking range, copper, also used for filling the bath tub in front of the fire a water closet, flushed by buckets and a walk-in pantry. The works office was located between the living space and the workshop. Two bedrooms occupied the first floor, access being via a winding stairway in the corner of a sitting room. All rooms, except the office, had their own fireplaces fitted with coal-burning grates. There was no heating within the workshop. Water in both workshop and house was obtained by hand-pumps from local wells, situated some 40 feet from the cess-pit."

GGJ Cooper, Paul Cooper's father, writing in 1995.

Quotes   :   GW Cooper (1867 - 1957)
Photos   :   GF Cooper (1896 - 1980)
Research   :   GGJ Cooper (1920 -   )
Compilation: GP Cooper (1950 -   )

Note - Geoffrey Cooper (GGJ above), has also produced *FARNBOROUIGH AND THE FLEET AIR ARM*. Published by Ian Allan in 2008. ISBN 978 857803068.

Opposite page - No 568 again. We cannot be certain if this was taken at the same time as the previous view although this would appear likely. In 1901 there were three local goods trains serving Romsey each way daily, on the route from Southampton to Salisbury or Eastleigh to Salisbury. There was also an additional service between Southampton and Andover. One goods train operated from Southampton on Sundays.

Above - 'Radial' No 419 in the cattle pens sidings, which were located on the down side of the line and at the east end of the station. The running lines are behind the engine. This was another engine that was duplicated, although the apparent lack of any indication to this effect on the cabside, may mean the date is prior to June 1904. Members of the class had been transferred away from the London area by this time and found work at various other depots including Eastleigh, no doubt where this particular engine was then stabled. This particular engine was subsequently seen working the Lyme Regis branch, but was condemned in November 1923.

Years later and with his grandfather now living alongside the GN main line at Biggleswade, Paul Cooper recalls spending many happy summer days at the lineside. "I remember him quite clearly explaining the 1955 Modernisation Plan to me as a 5 year old that would lead to the elimination of all steam engines. I think I took it on board but, at that age, it seemed a lifetime away."

SOUTHERN SHIPPING

Notes by Bert Moody

Above - '*DORSET COAST*',*(1,225g.t.) Built by, Ardrossan Dockyard in 1959 for Coast Lines Ltd. This photograph was taken at Folkestone between March and September 1965 when the vessel was on long term charter to British Railways for the cargo service between Folkestone and Boulogne. In 1979 Coast Lines sold the vessel to Egyptian owners and she was renamed 'EL HUSSEIN'. In 1981 she was renamed again, 'EL KHSER' and later the same year 'DENTON VENTURE'. In 1984 she was acquired by Greek owners and renamed 'OURANIA' and was broken up for scrap at Bruges in 1985.*

Opposite top - '*FALAISE*', *(3.7l0g.t.) Ordered by the Southern Railway from W. Denny & Bros Ltd of Dumbarton and completed in 1947. Accommodation provided -1,527 passengers and 30 cars, the latter lifted on and off by dockside cranes. Machinery consisted of four single reduction geared turbines driving twin screws. Until 1963 'FALAISE' operated on the Southampton - St.Malo summer service and at times during the winter on the Southampton - Le Havre service. In addition she made a number of short week-end cruises, mainly from Southampton. The photograph shows the vessel as originally built. At the end of 1963 'FALAISE' was sent to Vickers Armstrong yard on the Tyne for conversion to a stern loading, drive on/off car ferry. The accommodation was considerably altered and provision made for 700 passengers and about 100 cars, her gross tonnage was also reduced to 2,416g.t. She made her first, trip as a car ferry on the Newhaven - Dieppe service on 31st May 1964 and operated mainly on that service, although she was used on the Dover - Boulogne service. In 1973 she was transferred to the Weymouth - Channel Islands service. In August 1974 'FALAISE' was laid up at Holyhead and in December of that year she left under tow for Bilbao for scrap. Recorded on 11th November 1949.*

Opposite bottom - '*SHANKLIN*' *- The third of a group of three motor-vessels built for BR by W.Denny & Bros at Dumbarton for the Portsmouth - Ryde passenger service. 'SHANKLIN' was completed in 1951 with a gross tonnage of 833 and accommodation for a maximum of 1,370 passengers. In March 1980 'SHANKLIN' was withdrawn from service and in November of that year she was acquired by the Firth of Clyde S.P. Company, being renamed 'PRINCE IVANHOE'. The intention was that the vessel would support the paddle steamer 'WAVERLEY'. In April 1981 'PRINCE IVANHOE' commenced operating in the Bristol Channel area, but unfortunately on the 3rd August 1981 the vessel was wrecked in Port Eynon Bay, South Wales and became a total loss. Photographed 30th September 1956*

64

Opposite top - *'NORMANNIA'. Built by W.Denny & Bros of Dumbarton for British Railways service between Southampton and Le Havre. Completed in 1952 with a gross tonnage of 3,543. Accommodation was provided for 1,400 passengers. Machinery consisted of two double reduction geared turbines driving twin screws. In December 1963 'NORMANNIA' made heir final sailing on the Le Havre service and went to Hawthorn Leslie's yard on the Tyne for conversion to a stern loading drive-on / off car ferry. Her passenger accommodation was reduced to 500 passengers but provision was made for 111 cars. Her gross tonnage was also reduced to 2,219. In this form, she entered the Dover - Boulogne service in April 1964. In 1974 she was transferred to the Weymouth - Channel Islands service. Withdrawn from service in 1976 she was sold for scrap and broken up at Gijon where she had arrived on 6th December 1978. The photograph shows the vessel on 9th April 1964 and after conversion to a car ferry.*

Opposite top - *'LORD WARDEN'. Built by W.Denny & Bros at Dumbarton for BR for their Dover - Boulogne service. A stern loading car ferry completed in 1952 with a gross tonnage of 3,333. Accommodation was provided for 700 passengers and 120 cars. Machinery consisted of two double reduction geared turbines driving twin screws. During 1978 and again in 1979, 'LORD WARDEN' spent several weeks operating from Fishguard on the Rosslare / Dun Laoghaire sailing. At the end of 1979 she was sold to Baaboud Trading & Shipping Agency of Jeddah and given a short refit at Southampton, when she was renamed 'AL ZAHER', sailing from Southampton on 2nd January 1980 for the Middle East. She was broken up at Gadani Beach, Pakistan in May 1981. Photographed 15th May 1952.*

Above – *'LONDRES'. This vessel was ordered in 1939 for the Dieppe - Newhaven service, but before completion was taken over by the Germans and fitted out as a minesweeper under the name of 'LOTHRINGEN'. At the end of the war, the vessel was found at Kiel and returned to her builders at Le Havre for completion as a passenger ferry. She entered service in April 1947, with a gross tonnage of 2,444 and accommodation for about 1,450 passengers. Machinery consisted of six single reduction geared turbines driving twin screws. Ownership of the vessel was originally joint Chemin de Fer de L'Ouest and Southern Railway, but in 1955 she was taken over completely by British Railways. At the end of 1963 she was withdrawn from service and sold to Typaldos Bros Ltd of Piraeus and was renamed 'IONIAN II' for the voyage to Greece, but she was later renamed 'SOPOKLIS VENIZELOS'. On 14th April 1964, whilst undergoing a, refit in Piraeus, a serious fire occurred on board. She was beached outside the harbour and became a total loss.*

Preceding page - '*MAID OF ORLEANS*'. Another steamship built by W.Denny & Bros Ltd at Dumbarton for the Southern Region of British Railways. Completed in June 1949, with a gross tonnage of 3,772 and accommodation provided for 1,400 passengers. Machinery consisted of four single reduction geared turbines driving twin screws. '*MAID OF ORLEANS*' operated on the Folkestone - Boulogne and Dover - Calais services. In 1958/9 the top off her funnel was altered to keep the exhaust, clear of the accommodation This is shown on the photograph. '*MAID OF ORLEANS*' was laid up at Newhaven in 1975 and on 6th November 1975 left the Sussex port in tow of a Spanish tug destined for Santander and scrap.

Above - '*MAID OF KENT*'. Built by W.Denny & Bros Ltd of Dumbarton for the Dover - Boulogne service of the Southern Region. Completed in 1959 with a gross tonnage of 3,920 and accommodation provided for about 1,000 passengers and 190 cars. '*MAID OF KENT*' remained on the Dover service until 1974 when she was used on the summer service between Weymouth and Cherbourg until 1981. She was laid up at Newhaven at the end of 1981 and on 6th April 1982 left for a shipbreaker in Spain.

THE PROPOSED RAILWAY TO EAST WITTERING

Keith Smith

In August 1897, the Hundred of Manhood and Selsey Tramway (HMST) opened for business, transporting passengers between Chichester and Selsey at speeds previously unheard of! Steadily, the tramway increased its business and a notice in the Sussex Daily News of 23 May 1913 was the first indication to the general public that the tramway had ideas of expansion.

Passenger numbers had been steadily increasing - in fact, at the Annual General Meeting in August 1913, it was shown that the tramway had carried a record number of passengers, in excess of 89,000 in one year.

The public notice stated that the West Sussex Light Railway, under the Light Railways Act of 1896, had made an application for an extension to Itchenor and the Witterings. It set out the route in three parts; the first, Railway No. 1, to commence in the parish of Hunston via a junction with the HMST, at a point just south of the canal bridge crossing. It was to run in a westerly direction, following the southern bank of the canal, crossing the Birdham/Chichester road and then swinging towards Shipton Green. It would then continue towards West Wittering and cross Rookwood Road at the site now occupied by the Memorial Hall, then run directly across the fields to terminate in Church Road, East Wittering, where now St Peter's Roman Catholic Church is situated. The total length of the proposed railway was approximately seven miles.

Railway No. 2 simply related to the forked junction which would link Railway No. 1 to the existing Chichester to Selsey line, allowing access onto the new line from either Chichester or Selsey.

Railway No. 3 was to commence at Shipton Green and run in a northerly direction terminating just west of the Custom House at Itchenor. Here it was intended to build a 200' long reinforced concrete jetty where any vessel coming up the harbour could unload its cargo.

The total cost of building this new railway was estimated at just over £80,000 and a special meeting of West Wittering Parish Council was called on 12 June 1913 to discuss the project. The Parish Council unanimously agreed that the idea of connecting the village to the rest of the world would be a great boon. Mr W V Wray suggested that a railway would bring "an out of the way village such as West Wittering into the world and benefit the village educationally. The place ranks amongst the most beautiful seaside resorts in Sussex," he continued, "but it is little known and a railway will make it known. A result of the construction of a light railway would be an increase in the number of visitors, more houses would be built and the place would be livelier. It has been stated that it would be better to keep the place select, but I fail to see why our excellent front and fresh sea air should be the monopoly of the select. Let's look forward to seeing our beach in the near future with thousands enjoying the municipal blessings now enjoyed by other resorts in the county, including a West Wittering Municipal Band."

Following this meeting, a public enquiry was held in Chichester on 4 November 1913. It was well attended, with the promoters making much of the benefits that the railway would bring, especially to East Wittering, which was expected to develop into a seaside resort! There were some objectors, but after sitting for 2½ hours listening to the evidence, the commissioners were prepared to grant the Light Railway Order and they hoped it would benefit the district.

With the coming of the war in 1914, Government departments were very stretched and there was the inevitable delay in the order being sealed. Unfortunately, this did not happen until early the following year and by then public attention was directed towards the war and, despite increasing passenger

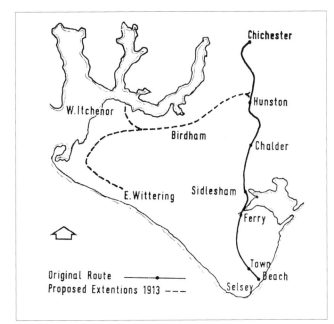

Original Route ——•——
Proposed Extentions 1913 - - -

numbers on the HMST, there seemed little enthusiasm for raising the necessary capital for the proposed new venture.

After the end of the First World War in 1918. much work was required on the original Selsey line. Money was short and the cost of living had increased dramatically. There were constant locomotive failures and unrest amongst the Board of Directors and to top it all, competition had arisen in the form of motor transport which proved to be quicker, cheaper and more reliable than the railway. Within a very short time, any enthusiasm for a railway to the Witterings had disappeared and the Selsey Tramway descended steadily into terminal decline, finally closing in 1935.

Would the Wittering branch line have made a difference, who knows? But we very nearly had a railway!

No. 24.

> Any further communication should be addressed to:—
> THE SECRETARY,
> LIGHT RAILWAY COMMISSION,
> SCOTLAND HOUSE,
> NEW SCOTLAND YARD,
> WESTMINSTER S.W.
> And the following letter and number should be quoted:—
> L 286.

LIGHT RAILWAY COMMISSION,

SCOTLAND HOUSE,

NEW SCOTLAND YARD,

WESTMINSTER, S.W.

11th.October, 19 13.

West Sussex _____ Light Railway.

Sir,

I am directed by the Light Railway Commissioners to acknowledge the receipt of your letter of the 10th, instant. forwarding a petition from the residents of East Wittering in favour of the above-named light railway, which shall receive due consideration.

I am, Sir,

Your obedient Servant,

ALAN D. ERSKINE.

Above - Locomotive 'Selsey' with a typical passenger train of the early years, heading south at Donnington. The spire of Chichester Cathedral is clearly visible in the background.   *Keith Smith Collection*

Left - Acknowledgment of the petition sent by Alfred Steel of the Royal Oak, East Wittering to the Light Railway Commissioners in 1913.   *Keith Smith Collection*

Below - 'Morous', a Manning Wardle 'Old Class 1' locomotive of 1866, works No 178, crossing Terminus Road Chichester with the up morning mixed train. Transferred on loan from the Shropshire & Montgomery railway in 1924, it became 'Selsey Property' (or West Sussex Railway as the tramway had by that time become) in 1931 for the sum of £50. The first vehicle is ex LCDR 6-wheeled brake second, SR number 3639, which the tramway acquired in late 1931. This photograph is interesting in that it shows the rarely photographed buildings at the extreme western end of the tramway's Chichester site. On arrival and after any passengers have alighted, the train will set back to leave the wagons on the line joining the Tramway to the main system ready for collection by an SR locomotive.

A P Kelly, Terry Cole Collection

The Ford Rail motor being guided across one of the line's ungated level crossings. The location in not given but is probably Stockbridge Road, close to Chichester. There is evidence of at least two passengers in addition to the Driver and Guard. The Ford Rail motor, which, together with the Shefflex Railcar, latterly ran all the non mixed trains, cost the company not a penny to purchase, as it was bought by Col Stephens himself.

A P Kelly, Terry Cole Collection

Keith Smith is, of course, co-author of the Middleton Press title *BRANCH LINE TO SELSEY*, as well as being involved with numerous other Middleton Press titles.

The Selsey Branch has also featured recently in a pair of book by Laurie Cooksey, published by Wild Swan. Other books on the same subject have been authored by David Bathurst and Edward Griffiths.

SCENES FROM 1950 to 1952

Photographs and notes by Jim Gosden

"On a Saturday in the Summer of 1951, chaos ensued at Walton-on-Thames, when a broken rail in Oatlands cutting between Walton and Weybridge, caused traffic routed on the down fast line to be diverted onto the down slow. The very first train to be diverted in this way then broke a coupling on the last carriage thus causing a total blockage of both down lines - a classic example of "Sod's Law".

"The aftermath was this scene at Walton-on-Thames, with 'King Arthur' 4-6-0 No 30450 'Sir Kay' on a down Salisbury waiting at the local platform and a 4-COR No 3127 on a Portsmouth service, waiting alongside. Most of the passengers appear to be waiting for news of some sort on the two platforms, also the driver of the 4-COR on the extreme left.

"The overall duration of the incident is not known, but from the time I arrived to discover the situation, I had time to cycle a mile home, get my camera, return and record the scene. About half an hour later, I was able to watch from Sir Richards's Bridge, half a mile away, as the steam service got under way, setting off detonators laid by the guard of the break-away train.

"As far as I can remember, there was no reporting of the incident on either the radio news (no TV news in those days), or, subsequently, in the London evening papers. Similarly nothing later appeared in the various railway periodicals.

"The disruption must have been pretty profound, with trains held in every block section back towards Waterloo. It was probably fortunate also that the incident occurred on a Saturday and not a weekday rush-hour. The whole saga was probably sorted in about two hours, which time included sending a steam engine, wrong-line, to collect the detached carriage, probably from Woking and the local permanent-way gang putting in a replacement rail from stock left close to hand".

Above - "I cannot recall ever seeing a photograph of any kind of a train on the Byfleet curve and certainly never on the curve proper. Presumably because only locals knew of the footpath which crossed the line to go to New Haw. 'S15' No. 30499 on a Southampton freight, 1951".

Left - "Oatlands cutting - referred to on the previous page, between Walton and Weybridge near to Oatlands signal box. I was able to get into the cutting through the back fence of the firm where I worked, the company having relocated from London to a large house and gardens at the onset of the war. The ends of the two long carriage sidings, referred to opposite top, can be seen, also St Richard's Bridge in the distance. The two signals were controlled from Walton-on-Thames and from memory of an official visit made to the box some years later in 1964, were motor operated.10201 on a Salisbury / Exeter working in 1951."

"Empty carriage stock from Waterloo was regularly sent to Walton-on-Thames carriage sidings for cleaning. The trains travelled via Clapham Junction, Richmond, Staines, Virginia Water and Addlestone, regaining the main line at Weybridge and appeared at Walton from the west on the up local line. At Walton, it was usual for the stock to draw into the up local platform, where the loco would take water. At this time, the usual class of loco was an 'M7' although sometimes it was a 'K10' or 'L11'. The stock would then be backed out of the station and down a long single line adjacent to the up local, to reach the carriage sidings. Each of these sidings could hold two 12 coach rakes, whilst a third siding could hold one 12 coach rake. Here the stock was washed and cleaned, both inside and out. During the war a hospital train in maroon livery and identified with the red cross against a white background, was berthed in the shorter siding. The vehicle immediately next to the engine, 'M7' No 667, is in the experimental 'plum and spilt milk' livery. (April 1950)".

"Summer 1951 at Walton-on-Thames. 'H16' No. 30519 on the 12.30 pick-up goods. After the necessary shunting, the train would leave around 1.00 pm, travelling to Feltham, via Addlestone".

"June 1951, Eastleigh shed scrap road. 'D15' No 483 is still displaying SR livery and is converted to burn oil fuel. It had been converted as such in September 1947 and was reported as having performed well. When the use of oil as a fuel ceased in October 1948, the engine was laid aside as seen here, although not officially withdrawn until December 1951."

'A12', 0-4-2, formerly 612, now DS3191, officially withdrawn in 1946, but subsequently in use supplying steam to the boiler yard at Eastleigh, a task it performed for four years from April 1947. "This view was recorded on an official visit to the works in June 1951, with the connivance of an apprentice of my own age, who was delegated to show me around the works. He kept watch, while I clambered on top of a spare boiler to get the only possible shot. June 1951"

"C14, 0-4-0T "Potato Can", makes an interesting juxtaposition with 34023 at Eastleigh in June 1951. Finally, '0415' 30584 at Axminster in June 1952 at Axminster in early BR livery but retaining Southern sunshine lettering."

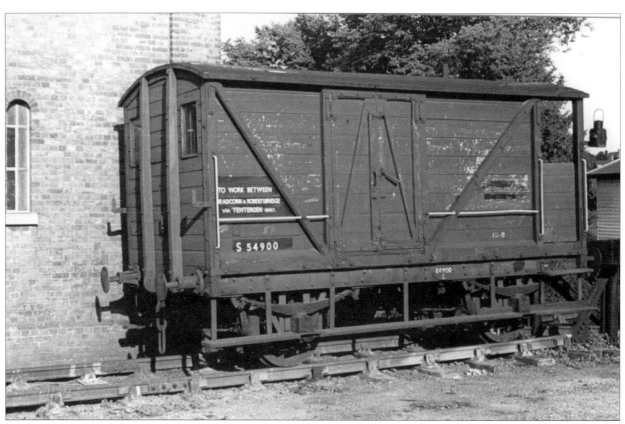

Terry Cole's Rolling Stock File No. 5
a trio of brake-vans

This time we take a look at examples of Goods Brake Vans from each of the three constituent companies of the Southern Railway. *Opposite top* - In this picture we see S54900, built by the LSWR and given SR Diagram no. 1541. Originally LSWR number 12439, it was one of 424 10 ton vans built to a William Panter design between 1887 and 1905. A further 20 vans up-rated to 15 tons were also built during this period, making this the most numerous pre-grouping brake van on the Southern Railway. These were single ended 'road' vans, with external framing and double doors each side to facilitate the loading and unloading of parcels and other traffic from intermediate stations. These vans were used throughout the Southern system and often branded, as here, for specific duties. This vehicle, which has recently acquired its BR number, is allocated to the Kent and East Sussex line and is seen here at Robertsbridge on 13/8/52. Examples of this long lived design were still in use until the early 1960s. *Opposite lower* - William Panter was the first LSWR Carriage and Wagon Superintendent. His son, Albert, after initially working under his father on the LSWR and a short spell elsewhere, became LBSCR Carriage and Wagon Works Manager in 1898 and LBSCR Carriage and Wagon Superintendent in 1911. The picture shows one of the 15 ton Goods Brake Vans he designed which were built at Lancing between 1915-1916. With heavy external framing, double side doors and single veranda, this could almost be an LSWR vehicle, with obvious similarities to his father's design of 30 years previously. 14 vans, SR numbers 55864 – 77, were built at Lancing to this design which was given SR Diagram no 1574. The corresponding LBSCR Nos. were 348 -361 and the Diagram was 24. This vehicle, number 5587 (the last digit is unclear), is seen at Norwood Junction Shed on 28/7/48. There was also a similar, but slightly longer, 20ton, 6 wheeled van to SR Diagram 1577. Unfortunately these vans did not last as long as those built by Panter senior and were generally withdrawn from revenue service between 1944 and 1950. *Below* - Here we see a totally different design of Brake Van, it has internal framing, a veranda at each end and 6 wheels. This is s 55434, one of 90 similar vans built by the South Eastern Railway / SECR from 1898 onwards. Rated at 20 tons, these vehicles carried SR numbers 55366 – 455 and were similar in appearance to some Midland Railway vans. The 40 original SER vehicles had a single veranda when built but were subsequently rebuilt to conform with the later vehicles, which had 2 from new. S 55434 is pictured here at Esher on 4/3/53. Most of these vehicles lasted into BR ownership.

And now an apology. In Issue No 3, I made an incorrect identification of the ex LSWR Brake Composite on the Hayling Island line and am indebted to Southern Way reader Peter Swift for pointing this out. The 3rd digit in the coach number is not very clear on the original print. After examining this under a glass I took it to be a 0, making the number 6404, which was indeed allocated to Haying Island around that time. I overlooked the underframe which quite clearly has LSWR trussing, not the SR underframe which rebuilds carried. A further close examination with the magnifying glass suggests the offending number is an 8, making the coach number S 6484. This would mean it is one of the 56ft Brake composites built by the LSWR in 1911-12, which became SR numbers 6481-6496 as suggested by Mr Swift. Both batches of coaches had similar passenger accommodation and layout.

I hope this sets the record straight.

Third Rail Items on the Southern, Part 2 - "Southern Conductor Rails"

After the last article on general conductor rail layouts, this article will move on to look at the next stages of connecting up the various elements of the conductor rail, mechanically and electrically.

Initially conductor rails were installed as fishplated rails using small two-hole fishplates. Fishplates and rails will be rust covered and therefore not give good electrical continuity at the joints, so good bonding around the joints is used to improve the electrical efficiency. In general, the head of the rail remains polished by successive train shoes, thus maintaining good electrical contact with the train. The first two pictures show equipment developed to ensure the conductor rail joints have as low an electrical resistance as possible. The braided copper bonds were forced into a pre-drilled hole in the foot of the conductor rail and expanded to fill the hole tightly. The pieces of equipment in both photos work on hydraulic pressure, created by good old fashioned arm power, the equipment being necessarily robust due to the forces involved in the process. The first photo (above) was taken in 1936; note the conductor rail here is slightly raised on the pots by temporary blocks. The horizontal press in the second photo is merely an updated version of the first one, the cylinder which is creating the force required being more obvious in this version.

Joints in the conductor rail form a mechanical and electrical weak point. So very early on, the advantages of forming rails as long as practically possible, between enforced breaks for expansion and electrical reasons, were seen as desirable. Conductor rails merely rest on the insulator pots, they are restrained at their mid-point, but free to expand on either side of this. The restrictions on allowable expansion ultimately limit the overall length of the conductor rail. Welding rails on site falls into three general types. The first is that used principally for running rails, namely the Thermit method, where a short piece of rail (typically 22mm) is cast between the two rails to be joined; however this is rare on conductor rails. The second method is to flash butt-weld the rails together. Here an electrical arc of high current/low voltage almost melts the rail ends which are held a short distance apart before they are forced together under high pressure creating a forged joint. This method is extensively used in a depot to create long lengths of conductor rails and running rails, as seen being delivered in the article in *Southern Way No 1*, though, in recent years purpose built road/rail vehicles have allowed this to take place on site.

The third method was to use gas-welding. This has now been replaced by manual metal arc-welding, but the process is similar and is used on site to join long and short lengths of rail together avoiding the need for fishplates and bonds as above. Portable plant, capable of providing the necessary power for arc-welding, had not been developed far enough in 1959 when these photos were taken near Paddock Wood, so melting the weld metal into the joint by high temperature oxy/acetylene welding equipment was the preferred method.

The process starts by grinding out a suitable vee in the head and foot of the rail, which is then re-filled with weld metal from the welding 'stick'. Tack welding the rail together with small surface welds is neither structurally solid enough, nor good enough to provide the required electrical continuity. The web (or middle portion of the rail) behind the fishplate, does not need to be welded, provided the head and foot of the rail are correctly fused. The train electrical shoe presses only lightly on the rail head and therefore the weld does not need the mechanical strength of a running rail weld.

This shows the welder carrying out the next process of filling up the ground out vee notches (the fishplate serving to align the rails for welding, they can be removed afterwards). The welder holds in his right hand a gas torch burning oxygen and propane, or oxygen and acetylene and in his left hand he is introducing the 'stick' of weld metal to the vee, literally melting it into the hot rail ends. On his right carefully arranged are some basic tools to assist. A cutting set, a 'flatter', a con rail spanner for the smaller fishplate nuts and the inevitable large ball-pein hammer.

Note he wares goggles against the very bright glare and welder's mitts or gloves. To get just the right height he has the comfort of sitting on a wooden box! How protective the trousers and groin protection are is hard to say, but the sparks would certainly burn and hurt! The overalls nowadays are flame retardant.

Having filled up the head vee and whilst it is still hot, the welder is now dressing the head with 'the flatter tool'. The head must be smooth for the shoe, which is effectively flat, to pass over. Ridges, misaligned or broken welds on conductor rail ends could catch a shoe and break it off. Sometimes all the shoes on one side of a train could be lost, thus preventing the train continuing where the conductor rail was on that side and causing serious and embarrassing delays. When the welder was happy with the head, he continued to fill the foot, 'dressing' the weld to provide good shape as he went.

The final weld would normally give unlimited service, mechanical strength to the joint and good electrical conductivity.

Apart from the substitution of manual metal arc welding for gas-welding, where a high current/low voltage electrical circuit through the weld rod to the electrical return via the rail introduces the weld metal to the vee, the process has remained relatively unchanged, taking typically two hours per weld to achieve. Nowadays the weld is ground to profile.

As the DC third rail system relies on a good electrical return path for the electricity to the sub- station, the return path via the running rails is also electrically critical. Running rails are often bonded together to ensure signalling circuits are reliable. This also ensures that the negative return path for the traction current is complete. In reality the system will still work with some poor bonding, the electrical current passing through items like fishplates. But every such situation increases the electrical resistance and affects the proper integrity of the system. The DC system is, essentially, a non-earthed system, requiring a good electrical path from the sub-station feed to the return collector at the sub-station. Electrical losses to earth points can cause unacceptable return paths to be created through pipes etc. leading to 'eating away' of component parts if left unchecked.

Therefore, from the beginning, it was realised that bonding rail ends together in a DC third rail system would avoid, as far as possible, the issues associated with poor electrical continuity.

This picture shows 'gas bonding' as it was known, where a braided metal strap was brazed to each rail head. The bond allows for small movement in the joint. These bonds, if carried out correctly, give years of useful life, being very firmly fixed and often difficult to remove when rails need changing! Other types of bonds were tried over the years with varying success. Nowadays short cables are used with bushes in the rail web, but the principle is still the same.

The tray arrangement below the bond and resting on the sleepers, is merely there to support the bond when it is welded on. This track uses BR3 baseplates on normal softwood sleepers, the rail being held by a hook arrangement on the outside of the baseplate, with spikes driven into round holes on the inside. These pictures were nearly all taken in the Tonbridge area in 1959 and much of this style of track still survives over the system. Over the years the sleepers age and the spikes come loose, so it is being eliminated by relaying. Similar styles of track using BR1 baseplates used spikes both sides of the rail. BR2 baseplates used a curly double spike known as a Macbeth spike. All have similar problems!

Health and Safety was also still in its early days; though the man does have goggles and a glove supplied, the rest he probably provided himself! He is holding the 'gas' torch in his right hand and the brazing rod in the left.

Electric comparisons, the old and opposite the new, which also leads us nicely in the article on page 91. The location above is the Ardingly branch - see note on opposite page. S7420S was part of a long line of mainly Maunsell vehicles, although there were some non-corridor items as well as 'Ironclads', displaced by the Kent Coast Electrification. The stock also changed from time to time as vehicles were removed for scrapping. (Roger Merry-Price has offered us a list of these vehicles for Issue 6.) Notice the route has been also been effectively singled. This took place with effect from 10.00 on Monday 19th May 1959, the former up line now a single line worked by the Electric Train Staff system between Ardingly and Horstead Keynes. The former down line thus became a siding. ETS was replaced by OES working in July 1962 and remained in this form until closure. Submitted by Roger Merry-Price / J J Smith - Bluebell Archive, additional notes by Martin Elms.

'REBUILDING' - THE LETTERS AND COMMENTS PAGE

First of all an apology. The last issue was so cramped for space there was simply no room for this section. Your comments, verbally, by telephone, e-mail and letter are appreciated and certainly all read. In no particular order then;

From Roger Thornton - who has pointed out the date for the view of the 'E1', page 99 'SW3' was 1st September 1963.

Several readers have passed comment over the cover view from 'SW4' showing the 'H16' at Clapham Junction. The consensus is they ran facing west due to possible tail swing at Waterloo. One also hit the buffers one day after the wheels picked up - water everywhere.

Fred Emery has suggested that the incident involving Mr Price (SW3), may have been due a works plate blowing off - behind which was high pressure steam. This was told him by an old driver who recollected that it had occurred near to Three Bridges, coincidence perhaps? On a totally different tack, Fred comments his late grand-father was one of the first men on the SR to drive a 'Nelson' when new. The story being that they rolled considerably compared with a 'King

Arthur'. As Fred points out though, this could of course have been due to the state of the permanent way.

Still on the subject of the 'Big Tanks', Eric Youldon has kindly submitted an article on these engines which it will be our pleasure to include shortly.

We have also received feedback from David Butcher (amongst others) over Paul Heathcote's piece on the run down of the S & D - (again SW3). The consensus is that all agree with Paul's conclusions over the underhand behaviour of the WR in this. Your comments have also been passed on to Paul who expresses his thanks. (Roger Merry-Price has also approached us with a promised article on S & D motive power and the discussion that took place between the LMR and SR in the 1950s'. We look forward to this soon.)

Slightly further back in time (SW2), and Douglas Hewitt has made mention of our comments re the proposal to fit a 'MN' boiler onto a 'Britannia' chassis. Doug has corrected us slightly, as it appears the true suggestion was in relation to 71000 'Duke of Gloucester', which would not steam at a rate of more than about 22,000 lbs/steam/hour. It was felt that if a

'MN' boiler was substituted all would be well, but impending dieselisation precluded any serious work being done on this. (As we now know of course, the problems with 71000 were in the end down to draughting in the grate, but this was not discovered until preservation.)

Eric Youldon has also passed comment concerning the recent Lymington, Waterloo and Devon Belle articles. So far as the fisrt is concerned, he does not believe the 'Pacifics' ever worked the Lymington trains, simply due to the turntable at Brockenhurst being too small. Coincidentally, Chris Richardson an ex Eastleigh Fireman, recently told us that you could turn a 'Standard 5' at Brockenhurst - just, it was very close and needed a good driver, but they did it several times, "...it saved running back to Eastleigh tender-first".

Eric continued that the 'M7' depicted on the second part of the Waterloo article cannot be No 125. The 'Devon Belle' article also incorrectly stated the banker was attached to the front of passenger trains at Exeter St Davids, it was only on freight workings that an assisting engine was ever attached to the front.

'SW4' included the view of the Midhurst train at Petersfield. Antony Hemens has added that the coaches have been retro-fitted with 1873 pattern destination board brackets and also that the board between the first two compartments on the first coach appears to be somewhat deeper than the post 1890 pattern.

Roger Merry-Price has advised us that the colour view of 31487 is not as stated but could well be Ashford. The view of 30915 is also possibly on the 'Kentish Belle', although more usual motive power at this time was a 'Standard 5'. (The location is also Bromley South with the rusty siding alongside running alongside the main line to Bickley.) The storage situation on the line from Copyhold Junction was such that over 100 carriages were located there, but only after the new sets destined for the Kent Coast electrification had been moved. Most of these stored coaches were believed later scrapped at Newhaven. Wagons were stored on the double track section north of Horstead Keynes.

Finally onto the 'Questions' feature relative to the Fawley working and the six wheel coaches. Several readers have advised us the need for two locomotives was due to the length of the train concerned, seven bogie vehicles and three 6-wheel carriages. The latter were ex LNWR vehicles transferred to the Southern for use as workman's accommodation at the time the refinery at Fawley was being enlarged. Further information on this can be found in John Fairman's book on the Fawley Branch published by Oakwood Press.

Thanks are also due to Peter Swift (Guildford) and Peter Swift (Derby), the South Western Circle, John Minnis, Alan Blackburn, Tony Woodforth, Tony Goodyear, Alan Butcher, Robert Barnes, etc etc.

As ever your contributions, whether it be a single photograph, article etc are all welcome. We cannot promise exactly when things will be used, but used they most certainly will be.

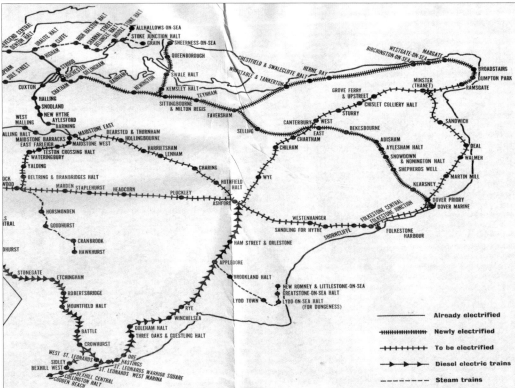

Mainstay of the new fast electric service were the 4 CEP units, a trio of which are seen displaying headcode 50, representing a Victoria to Ramsgate express, via Faversham.

The service is headed by unit 7139 which was delivered in February 1959.

THE KENT COAST ELECTRIFICATION

PHASE 1

June 15 2009 will see the 50th anniversary of the introduction of electric traction on the lines to Margate, Ramsgate and Dover. In the first of a two part article, Jeffery Grayer recalls the variety of new motive power introduced. The consequent effects on local steam traction and coaching stock being covered in the second part of this article.

The British Transport Commission gave approval for the Kent Coast Electrification (KCE) scheme in February 1956. The Kent Coast line to Ramsgate was felt to be a suitable candidate for electrification, as it was sharply graded, with much at 1 in 100 and many service slacks Its summer traffic was heavy and there was a substantial take up of season tickets by commuters from the coast to London. The former Southern Railway had planned to electrify the route and indeed got as far as Gillingham before the Second World War intervened, causing the remainder of the work to be postponed. It was decided to tackle the scheme in two distinct phases.

Phase 1 involved the extension of electric working from Gillingham through Faversham to Canterbury and Dover from Faversham to Ramsgate and Margate and covered the branch to Sheerness-on-sea. In all some 178 track miles were to be electrified, at a cost of £25m. Phase II, which would not be completed until 1962 and was estimated to cost a further £20m at 1959 prices, would fill in the gaps on a further 132 track miles, encompassing the lines from Dover to Ramsgate, from Ramsgate to Ashford via Canterbury, from Dover to Maidstone via Ashford, from Ashford to Sevenoaks via Paddock Wood and Tonbridge, and from Paddock Wood to Maidstone. In fact some parts of Phase II were completed 12 months ahead of schedule and electric trains began running from Sevenoaks to Folkestone and Dover and from Paddock Wood to Maidstone on 12 June 1961. The Folkestone Harbour branch was also electrified at this time.

In 1959 the only passenger lines outside the proposed electrified network were the steam operated branches from Gillingham to Allhallows-on-sea and Grain (Closed 4 December 1961), from New Romney to Appledore (Dieselised but Closed 6 March 1967), from Paddock Wood to Hawkhurst (Closed 12 June 1961), Dunton Green – Westerham (Closed 30 October 1961), plus the diesel operated lines from Hastings to London via Tonbridge (Electrified 1986), the branch from Crowhurst to Bexhill West (Closed 15 June 1964) and the Hastings – Ashford line. It was intended to include this latter line in the electrification proposals, but it was dropped due to concerns over the level of traffic likely to be generated.

Engineering works during Phase I were particularly heavy and involved the quadrupling of track between Bickley Junction and Swanley and between Rainham and Newington, with associated works at Shortlands and on the Bickley and Chislehurst loops. The majority of the platforms at Victoria were lengthened to handle 14 coach trains. A new electric locomotive shed was built at Stewarts Lane and the existing carriage shed was extended. At Shortlands the junction of the main and Catford loop lines was revised, raising the speed limits to 40mph and 60mph respectively. Speed limits elsewhere were also eased and platform lengthening at principal stations to take 12 coaches was undertaken. The provision of loops to enable fast trains to overtake slower ones was also made and the opportunity to introduce colour light signalling taken.

137 additional motormen and 68 electric locomotive drivers were selected from footplate staff for training at a new school opened at Stewarts Lane in November 1958. It was widely anticipated that Phase I of the electrification would spell the end of steam workings in the area affected, but, as we shall see in the second instalment of this article this was not to be the case.

The stock for the new service was to be provided by 43 four coach express CEP units (numbered from 7105), 10 four coach buffet sets BEP (numbered from 7003), and 63 two coach HAP units (6043 – 6105) . The CEPs/BEPs were developments of the 4 COR/BUF units introduced for the 1937 Portsmouth electrification. However, they used electro-pneumatic brakes and BR standard carriage designs. The BEPs were originally designated 4BUF (EPB), whilst the 4 CEPs were originally designated 4 COR (EPB). The designations stand for Buffet electro-pneumatic brake and Corridor electro-pneumatic brake. Prototypes of the new designs had entered service on the Central Division in 1956 with units 7101-7104 (CEP) and 7001-7002 (BEP).

The CEPs and BEPs were programmed to work the Victoria – Ramsgate/Dover fast trains, the chief Kent Coast business services and certain continental boat trains to Dover Marine. Although the KCE stock

Second Class Corridor Coach

This has eight compartments seating 64 passengers with a side corridor and toilets.

The compartment interiors are panelled in matt plastic and sycamore or ash, and a great deal of primrose plastic has been used to brighten the interior.

Shoulder lights above the seats are provided as well as the roof lights in each compartment.

Buffet Cars

Ten of the units have a buffet car in place of the second class corridor coach. These all-electric cars have a dining saloon seating 17 and a buffet-bar with kitchen and staff quarters in between. The kitchen equipment includes a refrigerator and ice cream chest and a special sterilising unit, as well as electric cooking devices and a stainless steel sink.

Intermediate Services

Sixty-two 2-car units, which can be run linked together to form anything up to twelve-car trains, have been built for the stopping services.

In decor they are not so obviously modern as the express stock. Each unit consists of one second-class semi-saloon divided equally into smoking and non-smoking accommodation for a total of 84 passengers. The other coach is arranged to provide 19 first class seats and a toilet in one part, and 50 second class seats, also with access to a toilet, in the other.

Because these units can expect to have much harder work trimming and decor are more orthodox—much like other post-war Southern suburban stock.

Interior of First Class Compartment ▶

Toilet	Non-Smoker		Toilet	Non-Smoker	Non-Smoker	Toilet
24 Second Class Seats	24 First Class Seats			64 Second Class Seats		

was based on earlier units of those types introduced in 1956 they included a number of modifications weighing in at an additional 3 tons. The axles and motors had roller bearings, the acceleration rate was slightly raised and oil-air operated, camshaft switches replaced the electro-pneumatic control gear. Only one motor coach had a motor generator and battery. The brake gear was re-designed and changes made in the bogies. The bodies were heat and sound insulated and fitted with double glazed windows. Plastic panelling was used internally, with aluminium racks and various patterns of upholstery. In service the double glazed units were found to admit water. They were subsequently replaced with single panes. After manufacture at Eastleigh, sets were stored at a variety of locations including Ford (Sussex), Barnham, Gatwick, Selhurst, Stewarts Lane, Bickley and between Ardingly and Horsted Keynes until required. At the latter location one line of the double track branch was used for stock storage. A Hastings based motorman was specially employed to extract each unit in turn, for running in on Victoria – Eastbourne services before replacing it at the rear of the queue, having moved the entire stock, which could be formed

of up to eight units buffer-to-buffer at any one time, in the meantime. The Horsted Keynes electric service perforce had to operate over a single line during this period. Some of the new sets were nabbed by the Central Division in the interim, to allow some of their elderly stock to be released for overhaul.

The HAPs would work other trains to Ramsgate and Dover and the Sheerness and Maidstone services. HAP denotes an electro-pneumatic braked 2 HAL unit (HAL denoting Half Lavatory). HAP's replaced HAL's, which up to Phase 1 had worked the electric services to Gillingham, Maidstone West and Sevenoaks. EPB (electro-pneumatic brakes) units, with their large seating capacity, formed into eight or ten car trains would also be used in the peak of the holiday season to handle the queues at those times at Victoria. While most of the four coach units were expected to be completed in time for the opening, it was thought that less than half of the two coach units would be available by the 15th June and this proved to be the case.

The delivery of KCE motive power is shown in the Appendix on page 96 from which it can be seen that not all units were in place by 15th June. Although all

CEPs and BEPs were delivered by June, units 7151-7153 did not enter traffic until July and six of them, originally intended for the KCE had been appropriated by the Central Division, to cover the increasing amount of time that their pre-war units spent out of service. Although HAP units were entering traffic only some 2-3 weeks after delivery, against the normal time of 4 weeks, there were still only 27 out of the 63 required available on 15 June. The shortfall in these units was made good by loans of HAL units. Only eight of the thirteen E5000 locomotives had been delivered by E-Day and Type 33 diesel locomotive deliveries were still several months away.

The various electric multiple units were supplemented by other types of motive power. Between 1959 -1961 ten motorised luggage vans MLVs were built at Eastleigh (S68001/2 for Phase I and S68003-10 for Phase II), to provide adequate space for the conveyance of the large quantities of luggage accompanying boat train passengers. Luggage and mail could be carried to the Channel ports under Customs seal in these special vehicles, which had to be motorised as using ordinary vans was ruled out, since this would have reduced the power-to-weight ratio of boat trains. Additionally, since luggage vans were traditionally marshalled at the rear of down boat trains, no driving position would have been provided at the front ends of up trains. There was also, of course, the problem of the 1 in 30 gradient on the Folkestone Harbour branch. Each MLV was powered by two 250 hp traction motors. They could also work over non-electrified sections, power being supplied at 200V from traction batteries which were re-charged via an auxiliary generator when the van ran on electrified lines. They contained motorman's, guard's, long and short luggage compartments, vestibule and motorman's compartments and were designed to haul 100 tons (limited to 50 tons up the Folkestone Harbour branch) as locomotives. These could

The pleasing lines of the new Bo-Bo electric locomotives are seen to advantage in this view of the Night Ferry, conveying wagons-lit sleeping cars and accompanying luggage vans on the English leg of the service from Paris. (From 1956 a portion to and from Brussels was included.) At Dover the sea crossing was via the Dunkerque train ferry. These locomotives remained in service until the last examples were withdrawn in 1977. E5001 is the sole survivor in preservation. The train itself was withdrawn on 31st October 1980.

Expresses

Fifty-three four-car units have been built for the express services running from June 15—the main line to Dover and Ramsgate via Faversham.

The units will usually be run in threes coupled together to form a twelve-coach train with a corridor running the whole way through. Two of the coaches in each unit will be second class open saloons which really do represent a new standard for second class travel on the Southern.

Outwardly they look much like the electric main line trains on other routes, but there is a hint here and there of a new brightness and gaiety.

Notice the bright curtains at the windows;

and the windows themselves which are double glazed, and larger than those on the older trains.

Inside the decoration varies with the type of coach but is always bright as well as practical. Plastic panelling—primrose, grey, blue, white and red—is used together with rich wood veneer, light wood framing and modern anodised metal finishes. The floor is covered with black marbled linoleum.

On the ordinary four-coach units there is a power coach (second class) at each end, which has open-plan seating, divided into two saloons by a centre glass panelled screen. These coaches seat 56 passengers in new style double-seats trimmed with a smart lined moquette.

Composite Corridor Coach

This has four first class compartments seating 24 passengers and three second class compartments seating the same number, as well as toilets at each end.

The second class compartments are the same as in the other corridor coach. In the first class compartments more wood finishes are used and the seats with their armrests and side quarters are trimmed in charcoal grey with a turquoise pattern.

Throughout all the cars the metalwork is finished either in anodised aluminium or silver-grey bronze.

◄ *Interior of Second Class Open Coach*

KENT COAST
Electric Train Services

London | Sheerness-on-Sea
Margate
Ramsgate
Canterbury
Dover

TIME TABLE June 15-Sept. 13 · 1959

SOUTHERN BRITISH RAILWAYS

---

consequently be used to haul local parcels trains.

Thirteen 2,500 hp Bo-Bo electric locomotives (E5000-5012) were built at Doncaster Works during 1959. Their role was principally the haulage of heavy freight and non-emu boat trains such as the "Golden Arrow" and "Night Ferry". Although they were fitted with pantographs for working in marshalling yards which had been equipped with overhead wires, they could not operate in non-electrified yards and the need to re-route them, often circuitously, when current was turned off for maintenance purposes over the electrified lines on which they were designed to operate, reduced their usefulness. Notwithstanding this a further ten were constructed in 1960. This shortcoming was not rectified until KCE Phase II with the prototype electro-diesels of Type 73 (E6001-6) which were equipped with a 550 hp diesel engine.

98 Class 33 diesel locomotives, mainly for freight on the Kent Coast and Hastings lines, were also ordered, 45 being scheduled for Phase I. However, delivery was retarded, with D6500 not putting in an appearance until January 1960, so in the interim the SR was loaned fifteen Type 24s, whose performance, even allowing for the difference in power, 1160hp as against

the 1550hp of the Type 33, was lacklustre to say the least, particularly at first when their use in tandem was banned. An added complication was the fact that they weighed 5 tons more than their designed weight so the SR Civil Engineering Dept banned their use on a number of routes where they would otherwise have been employed. A variety of adjustments were made to individual locomotives in a bid to reduce their weight, by removing train heating boilers or other fittings, or having them replaced with materials of a lighter weight. These actions resulted in two classifications being recognised, D5002-6 and D5001/7-14, the former having the greater freedom of movement. They were generally confined in their operations to Hither Green – Hoo Junction – Faversham and were not permitted to take on cross-London freights via the Metropolitan extension.

Towards the end of May 1959 the new electric locomotives and multiple unit stock were exhibited to the public at various locations, including Margate, Herne Bay, Ramsgate, Dover Priory, Canterbury West and Faversham, Whitstable, Sittingbourne and Sheerness. Trial running began in early June 1959 with the first electric service to run throughout from London

Victoria to Ramsgate being the 0800, hauled on 2 June by E5004 with nine coaches, followed on the same day by E5003 at 1510 and a 2000 departure to Dover Marine with E5004. Units 7138/41/42 formed the first emu train on 3 June from Cannon Street to Ramsgate. On June 9 a formal opening took place when Sir Brian Roberston, Chairman of the BTC and guests travelled by special electric train with units 7003/5 for a civic reception at Margate, returning at 1510 with unit 7004. The first public electric locomotive hauled train was the "Night Ferry" on 8 June with E5003.

In summary the new electric services provided a regular interval timetable as the publicity accompanying the new timetable indicated -

"The service is on a regular-interval basis. Hourly from 7-40 a.m. to 10-40 p.m, an express will leave Victoria, calling at Bromley South and Chatham (44 mins.) to Gillingham, where it will divide. The fast portion will continue non stop to Whitstable (75 mins.) and Herne Bay (81 mins.), calling at all stations to Margate (100 mins.) and Ramsgate (114 mins.) The second portion of each express will proceed to Sittingbourne, Faversham, Canterbury (88 mins.), and stations to Dover Priory (114 mins.).

"Also, at 40 minutes past each hour trains will leave Charing Cross for Woolwich, Dartford, Gravesend, Strood, Rochester, Chatham and all stations to Ramsgate. With the London expresses these will provide a half-hourly service between Herne Bay, Margate and Ramsgate, and a direct service between Gravesend line stations and the Kent Coast. Connecting with these at Faversham will be hourly stopping trains from Sheerness to Sittingbourne, Canterbury East and Dover. In addition, there will be hourly stopping trains from Victoria at 15 minutes past the hour to Sheerness, and the second portion of the expresses from Victoria, at 40 minutes past the hour, will have Sheerness connections from Sittingbourne, so that Sheerness also will have a half-hourly service from London.

"The fastest train of the day will be the 5-14 p.m. from Canon Street, calling only at Whitstable (65 mins.), Herne Bay (72 mins.), and stations from Margate (86 mins.) to Ramsgate (99 mins.), so for the first time on record providing a daily time of less than 1½ hrs. from London to Margate. On summer Saturday mornings and afternoons there will be a succession of eleven relief trains to the 40 minutes past the hour services from Victoria, with first stop at either

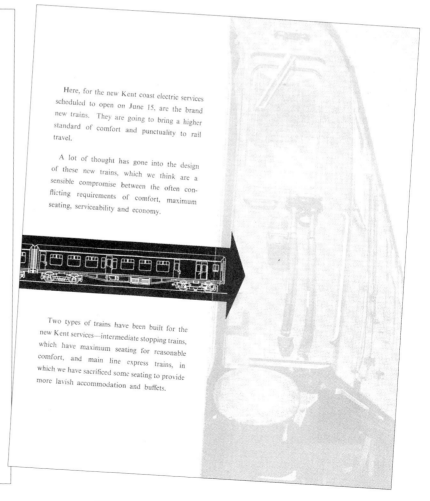

THE NEW SERVICES

The expresses run from Victoria throughout the day leaving at 40 minutes past the hour for Dover and Ramsgate. The trains will divide at Gillingham, one portion running via the coastal towns to Ramsgate and the other across country via Canterbury East to Dover Priory.

Up expresses will run both from Ramsgate and Dover Priory at ten minutes past the hour throughout most of the day.

Buffet cars will be provided on some of these trains.

The semi-fast trains leave Charing Cross at 40 minutes past the hour, calling at Woolwich Arsenal, Dartford, Gravesend Central, Strood and all stations to Ramsgate, and return from Ramsgate at 40 minutes past the hour. They are intended mainly for passengers only travelling along part of the route.

Semi-fast trains will leave Victoria at 15 minutes past the hour for Sheerness-on-Sea, calling at 14 stations on route. Trains in the other direction will leave Sheerness-on-Sea at two minutes past the hour.

There will be an hourly service between Sheerness-on-Sea and Dover Priory and between Sittingbourne and Sheerness-on-Sea.

The electrification to Dover and Ramsgate, together with very big engineering works to modernise and adapt the main route nearer London for the new services, has cost £25 million and taken two years. The scheme has included the installation of colour light signalling from Herne Hill to Ramsgate.

Now this is being followed with the electrification of the other main route to Dover (via Ashford and Folkestone) and the line from Dover round to Ramsgate. Similar rolling stock is to be built for this second phase of the scheme.

This is phase one of the Southern's complete switchover from steam on its busiest routes and is part of the British Railways Modernisation Plan.

Published by Southern Region of British Railways
Printed in Great Britain by Fosh & Cross Ltd.

AD8083/A25/1959

Here, for the new Kent coast electric services scheduled to open on June 15, are the brand new trains. They are going to bring a higher standard of comfort and punctuality to rail travel.

A lot of thought has gone into the design of these new trains, which we think are a sensible compromise between the often conflicting requirements of comfort, maximum seating, serviceability and economy.

Two types of trains have been built for the new Kent services—intermediate stopping trains, which have maximum seating for reasonable comfort, and main line express trains, in which we have sacrificed some seating to provide more lavish accommodation and buffets.

Whitstable or Herne Bay, two taking 87 minutes to Margate, two 88 minutes, two 90 minutes, one 91 minutes, one 93 minutes and three 94 minutes. A particular benefit for theatre-goers, will be the late evening expresses from Victoria at 10-40 and 11-50 p.m. to Herne Bay, Margate and Ramsgate. A connection from Faversham will be provided on Thursday nights to Canterbury East.

"Buffet cars will run daily in many of the expresses, at 40 minutes past the hour from Victoria, and the 4-44, 5-14, and 5-44 p.m. trains from Canon Street.

"The up service will follow the same pattern, with the hourly expresses leaving Ramsgate at 10 minutes past each hour from 9-10 a.m. to 10.10 p.m., and the connecting Dover service also at 10 minutes past. The journey time will be 115 minutes from Ramsgate and Dover, 102 minutes from Margate, 84 minutes from Herne Bay and 45 minutes from Chatham to Victoria."

So was the expenditure justified ? Some critics felt that the area to be served, a "geriatric coast" in some observer's eyes, would just not generate enough extra traffic to justify the investment, but in the first six months of electric operation some spectacular rises in ticket issues were reported – Rainham 300%,

Canterbury East 100% and Sittingbourne 40% leading to an overall increase in revenue of 27% rising to 32% after 9 months operation, proving doubts to have been unfounded. Theories that these exceptional rises were due to the good summer weather were disproved by the figure for November 1959, which showed an increase of 30% over the same month in 1958. The increase in travel was not confined to commuters, as the new shopping trains and late theatre trains also proved very popular, many of the theatregoers taking advantage of the combined rail and theatre tickets, which covered a number of London shows.

The chief downside, however, was the rough riding of the units, particularly the buffet cars, right from the beginning, a problem which got worse as mileage accumulated. Although there may have been some public over-reaction, in part spurred on by the press, the SR did admit that the riding of the new units was not up to standard, but attributed it to a very busy life over intensively used track, restricted clearances which affected the permissible displacement of the suspension and features inherent in emu stock. Some improvement was obtained through the substitution of Commonwealth bogies for the BR Mk 1 type beneath the trailers of the Phase II units, but in comparison with riding qualities of new stock elsewhere on BR the Kentish units were far from satisfactory.

Delivery of Phase I Kent Coast Electrification Stock								
Type	Delivered		Type	Delivered		Type	Delivered
Cl 71 (E5000-5012)			CEPs (7111-7153)			HAPs (6043-6105)	
E5000	12/58		7124-7127	12/58		6043	11/58
E5001	1/59		7129-7135	1/59		6044-6048	12/58
E5002	2/59		7136-7140	2/59		6049-6053	1/59
E5003	3/59		7141-7144	3/59		6054-6058	2/59
E5004	4/59		7145-7147	4/59		6059-6062	3/59
E5005	5/59		7148-7149	5/59		6063-6066	4/59
E5006	6/59		BEPs (7003-7012)			6067-6071	5/59
E5007	6/59		7003	3/59		6072-6077	6/59
E5008	7/59		7004-7007	4/59		6078-6086	7/59
E5009	8/59		7008-7012	5/59		6087-6096	8/59
E5010	9/59					6097-6105	9/59
E5011	9/59					MLVs (68001-68002)	
E5012	10/59					68001	4/59
						68002	4/59
						Class 33	
						D6500	1/60

COLOUR INTERLUDE

For this issue, we take as our theme the melancholy period of July and August 1967..

To many, this was the time the railway we had all known changed for ever, for the first time steam would no longer be running in parallel with electric traction on the Southern.

The scenes over the next few pages were recorded at Woking and Salisbury. At the latter location the engines might appear at first glance to be awaiting their next tour of duty, although closer examination reveals rods removed and rust beginning to show. Few would survive the journey to the South Wales scrapyards. 35030 above had been recorded 'dead' at Nine Elms on 22nd July, after which it was hauled to Salisbury and storage before disposal.

Even more poignant was the notice circulated in the week during the end of steam working on 9th July. After that date under no circumstances was steam power to be for any purpose. Perhaps Waterloo felt that in the event of a failure with the new order, someone might be just tempted……. Nice thought.

Photos by Maurice Hopper.

Opposite top - An unidentified 'Light Pacific' approaching Woking on the last day of steam working, Sunday 9th July. As well as the locomotive, Bulleid's coaching stock disappeared almost as quickly as his locomotives. The third to sixth vehicle also carry another dying tradition of the steam age, destination boards on the cant rail and roof.

Opposite lower - Two 'Standard' 4-6-0's, both in steam, head west from Woking, probably destined for Salisbury. They had been noted arriving tender-first earlier in the day from the Portsmouth line, meaning they had probably originated at Guildford.

Above - Salisbury yard some weeks after the end, when the Nine Elms allocation had mostly arrived to await disposal. As is known Eastleigh and Guildford were cleared first, indeed locally we all though there would be lines of withdrawn engines to be seen at Eastleigh for some time afterwards, but the shed was deserted by the morning of Monday 11th July.

Right - The products of Riddles and Bulleid.

Bulleid's and Standards, probably observed from a passing Hampshire diesel unit.

Issue No 6 of *THE SOUTHERN WAY* (ISBN 978-1-906419-13-4) should be available in April 2009

At the time of going to press we are hoping to include features on LANCING CARRIAGE WORKS, SOUTHERN WATER TROUGHS, 'SMOKE GETS IN YOUR EYES', further reminiscences from HUGH ABBINNETT etc etc - plus our usual features.

To receive your copy the moment it is released, order in advance from your usual supplier, or direct from the publisher:

Kevin Robertson (Noodle Books) PO Box 279, Corhampton, SOUTHAMPTON, SO32 3ZX

Tel / Fax 01489 877880

www.kevinrobertsonbooks.co.uk

We are also working on 'Southern Way Special No 3'

This is planned for late Spring 2009 and will feature the Southern alone between 1939 and 1942.